GERANIUMS &
PELARGONIUMS

GERANIUMS &
PELARGONIUMS

John Feltwell

COLLINS & BROWN

First published in Great Britain by Collins & Brown Limited in 2001
London House, Great Eastern Wharf
Parkgate Road
London, SW11 4NQ

1 3 5 7 9 8 6 4 2

British Library Cataloguing in Publication Data:
A catalogue record for this book is available from the British Library,

ISBN 1 85585 8452

Designer: Claudine Meissner
Editor: Corinne Asghar
Editorial assistant: Niamh Hatton

Reproduction by Global Colour Separation, Malaysia, Printed and bound in Italy

CONTENTS

INTRODUCTION

THIS BOOK IS ABOUT GERANIUMS — true geraniums, belonging to the geranium genus, and pelargoniums, that belong to the pelargonium genus. They are all popularly called geraniums, and they all belong to the same family. However, to aid interpretation in this book, the following guidelines have been adopted throughout.

The term 'geranium' refers to the genus Geranium, in which case it is in italics. If it is anglicized, members of the Geranium genus are called 'geraniums'. Similarly, pelargoniums are called 'pelargoniums' if anglicized, or of the Pelargonium genus if referred to in a botanical sense. Pelargoniums are never referred to in this book as geraniums.

The family to which both geraniums and pelargoniums belong is the *Geraniaceae* (or Geranium family). The members of this family are, in general terms, closely related to the family *Tropaeolaceae* (nasturtiums), *Oxalidaceae* (the Wood sorrel and Bermuda Buttercup family) and *Linaceae* (the flax family).

The family *Geraniaceae* has about 750 species scattered widely around the world growing as annuals, perennials, herbs and shrubs. Members of the family occur mostly in temperate and sub-tropical climates, in both the northern and southern hemispheres. Members of the Geranium family are generally absent from the band of tropical vegetation that straddles the world on the equator, with the exception of Africa. That pelargoniums occur across the Equator in Africa is not because they like tropical climates, but because they are only found there on high mountains and plateaux where the weather is much cooler. Pelargoniums have a preference for drier areas, since many are succulent, while some geraniums grow in the Arctic and Antarctic.

Characteristics of the family as a whole are that they tend to have jointed stems, often with glandular hairs, and their leaves may be simple or compound, sometimes with stipules. The flowers are usually regular, sometimes irregular often with nectaries. Flower parts are usually in fives,

---

TERMINOLOGY

The term 'geranium' is never used loosely in this book. it either refers to the genus *Geranium*, in which case it is in italics. If it is anglicized, then members of the *Geranium* genus are called 'geraniums'. Similarly, pelargoniums are called 'pelargoniums', if anglicized, or of the *Pelargonium* genus if referred to in a botanical sense. Pelargoniums are never referred to (knowingly) in this book as geraniums. These guidelines have been based on my background as a scientist and botanist.

G. phaeum
LEFT *A typical species geranium called the Dusky cranesbill shows off its upright nature whilst being resplendent in fine hairs that deter insect pests.*

P. 'Radula' AGM
ABOVE *This typical scented pelargonium shows the attractive arrangement of large and small petals with dark veining on the upper petals, seen in many pelargonium hybrids and cultivars.*

usually with five sepals, five petals, five female parts (ovaries) and five male parts (stamens) in two or three whorls. This is a basic structural plan of the flower, but there is much variation within the genera, as might be expected. Both genera have five petals and ten stamens. In Pelargoniums the petal number may be reduced to four or two, but the upper petals are usually larger than the lower ones. The similarity of the flowers of angel pelargoniums to violets and pansies is by chance; there is no connection between the *Geraniaceae* and *Violaceae* families.

There are eleven genera in the *Geraniaceae* family, of which pelargonium and geraniums are covered in this book. These two belong to one of the four sub-families called the *Geranioideae*, of which there are three other members, *Erodium*, *Monsonia*, and *Sarcocaulon*.

SIMILARITIES AND DIFFERENCES

There are large differences between geraniums and pelargoniums. In addition to botanical differences, in Australia and the US geraniums are what are described as zonal pelargoniums, and regal pelargoniums are called geraniums. Pelargoniums have thick, succulent stems and are mostly frost-sensitive, dying during the winter period if not brought inside for protection. Geraniums have more delicate stems and are mostly frost-hardy, often dying to ground level but reappearing in the spring. Both groups can be grown from seed, although many pelargoniums are produced from cuttings. Geraniums are grown exclusively from seed and many are perennial.

Few geraniums are grown indoors, whereas pelargoniums make fine houseplants. Pelargoniums have a recognizable, pungent scent, but most geraniums are unscented.

Pelargoniums have captured the imagination of breeders for over 200 years and several thousand cultivars have been produced; geraniums have remained more species-based and there are fewer hybrids among them.

There are many similarities to consider as well. This is a reflection of their family connections. The reason for confusion between geraniums and pelargoniums is that there will always be an overlap when man-made

The Montpellier Botanic Garden, Hérault, Southern France
BELOW *This is where many 'geraniums' (pelargoniums) were grown and observed, and where Augustin-Pyramus de Candolle (Director in 1808) gave his name to the* Myrrhidium *and* Peristera *sections of pelargoniums. The* Jardin des Plantes *is still an excellent place for studying pelargoniums because of its Mediterranean climate, especially its long hot summers.*

classification is used. There are geraniums that look exactly like pelargoniums with typical soft felted stems and large rounded leaves. These are classified as *Geranium potentilloides* – which refers to a pelargonium masquerading as a geranium. The plant grows in the Temperate House of Kew Gardens in London and has been verified as being South Australian in origin with a range emcompassing temperate Australia, New Zealand and Tasmania.

However the biodiverse world of geraniums and pelargoniums has speciated, and however man has chosen to select albinos, forms, varieties and hybrids, the world of 'geraniums' is sufficiently large for the gardener to pick and choose certain gems and to find areas of personal fascination. I trust you will find sufficient interest within these pages to indulge this passion and maybe expand your horizons.

The colour of the flowers is also similar, particularly pinks, reds and whites. The plants' habits share some similarities as well. Many pelargoniums and geraniums produce good bushy growth, which contributes to their continued popularity with gardeners around the world. Geraniums work well for groundcover, while pelargoniums are perfect for bedding, containers or even for creating carpet bedding.

Erodium pelargoniiflorum
ABOVE *Sharing the family looks, this* Erodium pelargoniiflorum *is named after its pelargonium-like flowers. The flowers have the typical darker markings on the upper petals, seen in so many pelargoniums, from the petite decorative angels to the magnificent regals. The species is native to Asia but it could easily pass as a pelargonium.*

GERANIUMS

ERANIUMS AS HARDY perennials are one of the prettiest and fanciest of the wild geraniums to grow in the garden. Starting from a wide range of wild species that come with all the hardiness you might expect from species that have to tough it out in exposed mountainous conditions, there is now a huge range of cultivars and hybrids selected by plantsmen which can meet the needs of all gardeners. Their delicate petals, and the amazing variety of colours available, add to their overall appeal.

G. sylvaticum
ABOVE *The Wood Cranesbill is a good mixer. Here, giant alliums help the Wood Cranesbill in its quest for light. It will tolerate dappled light, so does well in orchards and around the edges of woods and hedges.*

G. wallichianum
LEFT *Named after surgeon and botanist N. Wallich, this species is native to the Himalayas, Kashmir and Afghanistan. It can be grown in herbaceous borders or rock gardens and flowers from July to October.*

INTRODUCTION

Wild geraniums found in gardens range from the popular to the connoisseur's species cranesbills. The virtues of gardening with wild geraniums are that they are equally at home in rockeries, alpine gardens, beds, borders and wildflower gardens.

DESPITE THE SIMILARITIES and differences explained on previous pages, wild geraniums all have one obvious characteristic, a long and pointed fruit that looks like a crane's bill. This is reflected in the Greek word for crane, 'geranos' which has given us the word 'geranium'. What also separates them from the pelargoniums are the leaves that are mostly divided into five, each of which is then much indented. Thus the wild geranium leaf is highly characteristic and is often used as an identification feature.

In case there is any shadow of doubt over the geranium name, in this section of the book all the species and cultivars that belong to the genus Geranium are called wild geraniums. This section is therefore not about plants popularly called 'geraniums' (which belong to the genus *Pelargonium)*, but about plants that are otherwise called 'true geraniums'.

There are about 400 named wild geraniums known and they are all called by their genus name of *Geranium.* Wild geraniums occur on most continents, but like pelargoniums they avoid the sub-tropics and tropics. Many are species wild geraniums and live in mountainous areas, often in thin stony soils and ravines. Others live in lush alpine meadows and marshes, or in light woodland or along the woodland edges. Both uplands and lowlands support wild geraniums, and many have spread on different continents as weeds.

Wild geraniums are hugely successful at exploiting newly disturbed ground, where propagation is by seed expulsion from the 'cranes's bill' and subsequent dispersal by wind. This means they are opportunistic and well able to colonize new ground. This feature is well exploited in the garden where they can become dominant and will need some restraint by division. According to the species or cultivar, wild geraniums are either annuals, perennials or, rarely, shrubs.

Most wild geraniums are hardy perennials and make important contributions to the long-term structure of the garden. The shape of mature specimens of wild geraniums is useful in the garden, for they can very loosely be classified as two types according to their growth habits: first, those that grow in a mounded or hummock fashion, and those that grow tall, sometimes with an open rosette at the base. Both of these are fundamental elements used in every garden designer's plans. Once in the garden these perennials can take over, and, as one tabloid newspaper selling geraniums said recently of 'Wargrave Pink': 'It gives superb ground-cover and stops weeds dead in their tracks'.

There is no doubt that many of the world's wild geranium species have been brought back to the garden for enjoyment, and many of these wild geraniums can still be seen in their native locations. In fact some

G. × oxonianum 'Old Rose'

ABOVE LEFT *Smaller than other cultivars, this has very variable reddish-purple flowers that become darker with age. Another distinctive feature is the strong veining on the petals.*

G. × oxonianum 'Thurstonianum'

ABOVE *The narrowness of the petals is the feature that distinguishes this cultivar. All derived as clones from 'Claridge Druce', the plants are large and vigorous with lots of reddish-purple flowers.*

G. 'Johnson's Blue' AGM

ABOVE *One of the long-time favourites of the herbaceous border where it makes mounds of vegetation with its divided leaves, this cultivar has very distinctive blue petals. It is in flower from mid-spring to late summer and can be propagated by division.*

G. endressii AGM

LEFT *Of widespread occurrence and popular for its reliable pink flowers and low cover of vegetation, this species takes its name from the German botanist P.A.C. Endress. At home in borders in full sun, it also grows well in woodland glades and in wildflower gardens.*

species are so naturally dominant in their natural habitats that they have become highly visible signature species of those localities. For instance, the Bloody cranesbill is both a signature of the Yorkshire and Derbyshire Dales in north England and of The Burren in County Clare in Western Ireland. In both cases the species abounds on limestone and makes a living in the well-watered, but fast-draining crevices and fissures. This does not mean that you can grow Bloody Cranesbills only on limestone, it is far more tolerant of different conditions. On Madeira the giant Madeiran Cranesbill is a roadside casual, some having migrated from steep volcanic slopes where the disturbed ground provides the same type of stony habitat.

Growing wild geraniums in the garden is therefore relatively easy. They will take advantage both of the richer conditions in the garden, and, if forsaken in a dry urban back garden, will equally prosper. Gardeners wishing to get started with wild geraniums may wish to know that many geranium species and cultivars are quite resistant to pests and diseases and are ideal for beginners.

One of the first to collect geraniums from the wild seriously was Carl Linnaeus who called them all geraniums. Most in fact were what we now call pelargoniums (as it is anglicized it is in lower case), but they were all called geraniums then. His work is described in this book in the Pelargonium section.

EASY SPECIES AND CULTIVARS

The following are a short selection of easy-to-grow geraniums for the garden

G. cinereum 'Ballerina' AGM	G. endressii AGM	G. pratense
	G. himalayense	G. procurrens
G. cinereum 'Lawrence Flatman'	G. 'Johnson's Blue' AGM	G. psilostemon AGM
	G. macrorrhizum	G. sanguineum
G. clarkei x collinum 'Kashmir Purple'	G. x magnificum AGM	G. sanguineum 'Nigricans'
	G. nodosum	
G. clarkei x collinum 'Kashmir White' AGM	G. x oxonianum	G. sylvaticum
	G. palustre	G. versicolor
G. collinum	G. phaeum	G. wlassovianum

Linnaeus's collection of wild geraniums is fascinating, not least because some of the colour of the flowers in these herbarium specimens are still visible after 250 years. Pink flowers of *G. pyrenaicum* are still remarkably preserved and the flowers of Bloody Cranesbill have only dulled to a brown colour. Shut away for most of their life in the dark it is likely these colours will survive for a couple more centuries to come.

More than 100 years later Robert Sweet, who became a Fellow of The Linnaean Society which housed Linnaeus's specimens, wrote what is now a classic book on the 'natural order' of the geranium family. His volumes, printed in 1824-1826, are filled with the most exquisite colour pictures of both pelargoniums and geraniums, which are still lively 160 years on, and are better colour-printed than many gardening books of today. All his wild geraniums are given common names as well as their Latin ones, and the English names are usually a direct, if not obvious, translation, from the Latin. Many of the English names have been lost. The list in the box above indicates the species that were available to him, all of which are available today.

The virtues of gardening with wild geraniums are great in both the northern and southern hemispheres in temperate and Mediterranean climates. In the garden they are best suited to the herbaceous border or the wild garden either in a meadow mixture or as marginal vegetation bordering a woodland walk or in an orchard, either in the full sun, in dappled light or in shade – they really are very accommodating. *Geranium endressii* AGM is very good as a groundcover plant and does well in shade.

G. pratense

LEFT *Here the Meadow Cranesbill is mixed with Lady's Mantle* (Alchemilla mollis) *at the front of the herbaceous border in a complementary association that helps to support the cranesbill.*

G. pratense
LEFT *This herbarium specimen was collected in the mid-18th century and was part of Carl Linneaus' collection. Linnaeus was the Swedish botanist who gave universal Latin names to plants and animals. This specimen still shows off its petal colours, albeit faded, more than 250 years later. This is mainly due to the herbarium specimen being conserved in the dark at a constant cool temperature. The five-fingered arrangement of the leaves is typical of the geraniums that have many lobes and sub-divisions based on this design.*

Small wild geraniums can be slotted into cracks in patios or chinks in walls where they will often perform better in the warmer conditions. In the wild many geraniums eke out an existence on a vertical surface in preference to stony ground. The advantages are better drainage and greater warmth. Few gardeners try to emulate the natural habitat of wild geraniums and there is much room for experimentation. Other wild geraniums are suited to the traditional rockery, or the more popular scree bed, and there are yet others for connoisseurs to nurture in an alpine house. The variety of wild geraniums found in gardens ranges from the popular to the connoisseur's species. The virtues of gardening with wild geraniums are that they are equally at home in rockeries, alpine gardens, beds, borders and wild places.

WILD GERANIUMS

named by Robert Sweet in the 1820s
(following his own classification and spelling)

Erodium incarnatum (syn. G. incarnatum)	Flesh-colored Heron's-bill
Geranium anemonefolium	Anemone-leaved Crane's-bill
Geranium argenteum	Silvery-leaved Crane's-bill
Geranium ibericum	Iberian Crane's-bill
Geranium lividum	Wrinkled-leaved Crane's-bill
Geranium macrorrhizum	Long-rooted Crane's-bill
Geranium multifolium	Multifid-leaved Crane's-bill
Geranium nepalense	Nepal Crane's-bill
Geranium palustre	Marsh Crane's-bill
Geranium Vlassovianum	Vlassof's Crane's-bill
Geranium wallichianum	Wallich's Crane's-bill
Pelargonium bicolor (syn. G. bicolor)	Two colored Heron's bill

INTERNATIONAL GERANIUMS

North America relies heavily on introduced species from Europe and Asia. Species such as *G. dalmaticum* AGM, *G. endressii* AGM, *G. macrorrhizum*, *G. phaeum*, *G. pratense* and *G. sanguineum* are familiar to gardeners on both sides of the Atlantic. Some varieties of the Dusky Geranium are available in North America, but not apparently in Europe; these include *G. p.* 'Chocolate Chip' and *G. p.* 'Langthorn's Blue', whereas *G. p.* 'Calligrapher', 'Mourning Widow' and 'Samobor' are available on both sides of the Atlantic.

Cranesbills fit beautifully into the herbaceous borders of New England where the climate is comparable to the Atlantic climate experienced by gardeners in England. On the west coast of America cranesbills also complement borders, but in the south west the hot landscape makes them more difficult to grow successfully. The Mediterranean climate of the west coast brings out the best in these plants under the right conditions. Gardening under trees serves geraniums well so they often thrive where homes have been built in leafy situations.

In the southern states such as Mississippi and Alabama, cranesbills species hardly appear in books on perennials because introduced species and cultivars cannot tolerate the hot, humid conditions. In wild gardens, however, the native North American *G. maculatum*, or Wild Geranium, can be grown in stony sites and on scree beds mimicking its natural habitat. Do not confuse wild geraniums with *Saxifraga stolonifera*, also called the Strawberry Geranium.

Good growing conditions for most wild geraniums exist on the western seaboard, and most mature plants can survive in temperatures as low as -10°C (14°F), and sometimes even colder. The exceptions to this rule are the large western Atlantic geraniums such as *G. canariense*, *G. maderense* AGM and *G. palmatum* AGM, and many of the South African cranesbills such as *G. incanum*. *G. incanum* is a trailing geranium which has finely cut leaves and can be grown as groundcover. It has magenta pink flowers but it is frost-sensitive and so can only be grown in warm climates. *G. traversii* is a frost-sensitive wild geranium whose lower limits are about -6.6–3.8 °C (20–25°F).

CRANESBILLS IN UNITED STATES OF AMERICA AND AREAS OF HARDINESS, ACCORDING TO THE UNITED STATES DEPARTMENT OF AGRICULTURE (USDA) CLIMATE ZONES

The hardiness of each cranesbill in the USA has not yet been ascertained, so this list is drawn from several sources. There are also differences of opinion regarding hardiness. There are two factors to consider: first, the aspect of your garden – you might have a warm site with hot spots that will notch up another zonal area; second, young plants are more tender than mature specimens. Most cranesbills are hardy perennials, many of which hide underground for winter.

Species or cultivar	USDA Climate zones
G. 'Ann Folkard' AGM	zones 5-9
G. x cantabrigiense	zones 4-9
G. cinereum var. subcaulescens AGM	zones 4-9
G. clarkei	zones 3-9
G. dalmaticum AGM	all zones
G. endressii AGM	zones 4-9,
G. himalayense	zones 5-9
G. 'Johnson's Blue' AGM	zones 4-9
G. macrorrhizum	zones 3-9
G. magnificum AGM	zones 4-9
G. phaeum	zones 3-9
G. pratense	zones 2-9
G. psilostemon AGM	zones 5-9
G. sanguineum	zones 4-9
G. wallichianum 'Buxton's Variety' AGM	zones 6-9

G. macrorrhizom 'Variegatum'
OPPOSITE *The edges of this old favourite have attractive cream margins. This tall plant creates an interesting variation in a herbaceous border.*

G. x wallichianum 'Buxton's Blue'
ABOVE *One of the most striking of the perennial wild geraniums, this hybrid typically has a pretty light eye within the outer blue ring.*

In the Pacific Northwest and the coastal areas of California there are three cranesbills which perform particularly well. These are the attractive *G. wallichianum* 'Buxton's Variety' AGM, which has a long flowering period, the popular *G.* 'Johnson's Blue' and *G.* × *magnificum*, whose unusual leaves glow red in autumn.

The 'black-eye magentas' are especially good for growing in borders. The tallest of these is *G. psilostemon*, which grows to over 1m (3ft) high. It can be mixed with a variety of species such as foxgloves (*Digitalis* sp.), astilbes (*Astilbe* sp.) or goatsbeard (*Aruncus* sp.). The red and black-eyed *G.* 'Ann Folkard' AGM is resplendent with its young yellow leaves, while *G. cinereum* var. *subcaulescens* AGM grows closer to the ground and is therefore ideal for use at the front of the border or in rock gardens or as edging to paths where it can be mixed with a variety of plants, such as white-leaved salvias or *Lychnis* sp. candytuft (*Iberis* sp.) or irises. Use *G. cinereum* 'Ballerina' AGM or *G. cinereum* 'Lawrence Flatman' for softer flower shades.

Antipodean Cranesbills

Evolution and natural selection may have favoured cranesbills with their epicentre of distribution in Turkey or in China, but there are few native cranesbills in Australia and New Zealand. Many cranesbill species were, however, introduced from Europe. Settlers were eager to set up their own gardens in the English genre with species from Europe, it is highly likely that a large amount of trade was done with wild geraniums over the years. Virtually all the familiar geraniums of English gardens will grow in Australia, that is in the warmer lowlands rather than the desert, but especially where a Mediterranean climate exists along the southern coast.

There are not that many Australian species that have made it into gardens elsewhere in the world, but *G. sessiliflorum* subspecies *novae-zelandiae* is one them. It is native to both the north and south islands of New Zealand and it exists in two leaf colour forms, green and dark bronze, called *G.* subsp. n. 'Nigricans'. There are two other subspecies, *sessiliflorum* in South America and *brevicaule* that occur both in Tasmania and the southeast highlands of Australia. *G. sessiliflorum* grows to about 7cm (2 ¾ in) and produces cushions of tiny white flowers on a rosette of small rounded green leaves.

FLOWERS

Geranium flowers range from tiny to about 2.5 cm (1in) across, and through a range of colours from blue to reddish-violet. Because of their beautiful flowers, geraniums play an important part in the sequential color of herbaceous borders.

WILD GERANIUM FLOWERS are all regular in that they have five petals and five sepals. The petal colour ranges from white through pink and purple, purple-red, and blue, and the shape of each petal is usually rounded at its extremities. The flower is often saucer-shaped but it can also be star-shaped as well. The petals may be flat or reflexed. At the base of each petal there is a nectary which produces a sugary nectar. For this reason honeybees and bumblebees find wild geraniums very attractive and will flock to your garden if they are planted.

There are always five sepals and these are usually green and hairy. At first they enclose and protect the bud before the petals open, but when the fruit develops they enlarge, change colour, and protect the base of the huge developing fruit.

The reproductive elements are made up of male and female parts found in each flower. There are ten stamens, or male parts, some short, some long, making up a whorl of stamens with their accompanying anthers in the centre of the flower. The anthers produce pollen. The female part comprises the stigma, style and ovary enclosed with the stamens. It is the stigma that receives the pollen that then grows down the style to fertilize the ovule in the ovary.

The individual flower is often borne on a long stalk, sometimes in clusters, which is a reflection of the natural habitat in which wild geraniums grow. Many live in long meadow grass and have to compete with other tall species, thus their nodding flowers on long stalks, or clusters of flowers, succeed in reaching the sunlight. Their

G. asphodeloides
LEFT *Native to the eastern Mediterranean this species has rather pinched-up sepals. It exists as three distinct subspecies, named subsp.* asphodeloides, crenophilum *and* sintenisii, *that vary in stature and leaf structure. The species acts as a biennial or perennial.*

G. 'Dilys'
LEFT *The product of a cross between the Bloody Cranesbill and G. procurrens, this hybrid is named after Dilys Davies of the United Kingdom's Hardy Plant Society. It grows as a mounded plant up to 23cm (9in) and spreads to about 91cm (36in).*

G. 'Sue Crüg'
ABOVE *Looking resplendent with its strong purple petals, this cultivar has a characteristic tubular shape and reflexed petals. The petals are heavily marked with veins and the leaves are strongly divided.*

G. pratense 'Plenum Caeruleum'
RIGHT *The Latin name means 'double blue' and this cultivar has an attractive blue hue to enhance a border. Like its many related cultivars of the Meadow Cranesbill it does well in sunny positions.*

use in the herbaceous border to give height in the mid-range is obvious. Other species have a more sprawling habit and their flowers are borne on short stalks, albeit on long stems in order to cover the ground. These are especially suitable for use in rockeries. Some double-flowered wild geraniums have been produced, notably G. 'Southcombe Double'.

Many of the wild geranium species that are not much grown in gardens, except wild or naturalistic ones, have tiny flowers in relation to a large amount of stem and leaf growth, such as *G. robertianum*, *G. dissectum* or *G. pyrenaicum*. Tiny flowered cultivars include G. 'Nimbus'. It has one of the brightest magenta flowers of any wild geranium species and is useful for producing bright centres of colour in otherwise very shady places.

Flower colour is conservative, having evolved mostly in the pink and purple range, but with a good range of blues (G. 'Buxton's Blue', *G. wallichianum*). Naturally there are albino forms of a number of species and these have been promoted in cultivation (*G. sanguineum* 'Album' AGM).

There are also species that are white in their own right (*G. albiflorum*). Two characteristics have been selected in hybridization – first the tendency of the petals to have faint netting running along the length of the petal has been improved, as in 'Lace Time' and, second, the base of the petals has dark pigmentation resulting in the whole flower having a dark eye in the centre, as in the hybrid G. 'Ann Folkard' AGM, G. 'Patricia' or *G. kurrodo*. *G. cinereum* 'Ballerina' AGM has both characteristics – pronounced veins with a dark eye.

When the flower is pollinated the petals fall off since they are not needed to attract any more insects. The ovary of each flower has ten cells each containing two ovules. When fertilized the ovules develop into seeds and the remains of the flower, including the reproductive parts become fruit. Maturation of the ovary results in a long and pointed ripe fruit. When dry and ready to distribute its seeds, the sides of the fruit twist and shoot out the seeds. Seeds can be collected when ripe and sown straight away or in the following spring, outside or under glass or plastic.

G. cinereum 'Ballerina'
ABOVE *This attractive and popular hybrid is a result of crossing two subspecies,* cinereum *and* subcaulescens. *The dark centre of the flowers is accentuated by the purple petals shot with dark veins.*

G. pusillum
RIGHT *The flowers of this annual species are small and borne within a mass of foliage whose leaves are finely divided. Even 'weedy' species such as this are attractive and may be grown in a wild garden for curiosity. It is native to Europe and Asia.*

G. pyrenaicum
LEFT *Small but beautiful, the white or pink flowers of this species help to liven up woodland edges and hedgerows. It is happy growing in dappled shade.*

G. × rivers-leaianum 'Russell Prichard' AGM
LEFT *The brightly coloured flowers of this hybrid are always an attraction in a garden and its virtue is that it is long-flowering.*

G. × riversleaianum 'Mavis Simpson'
ABOVE *The petals are crumpled slightly at the edges and decorated with thin veins of deep purple.*

G. koreanum
LEFT *A species geranium from Korea, as its name suggests, the flowers have widely-spaced petals around the floral parts.*

FOLIAGE

Wild geraniums make a big contribution to foliage in the garden and anyone contemplating including some foliage should consider using wild geraniums, not least because of their fiery autumn colours.

A GREAT DEAL OF the beauty of wild geraniums is in the leaves. As hardy perennials they spend a lot of the time out of flower with just their leaves to look at, but these are as diverse and beautiful as they are functional.

In the wild, geraniums tend to cover their patch thus securing for all the nutrients and water they can extract from the soil using their large leaves.

While wild geraniums are flowering, their mounds of foliage can be very attractive, such as the silvery leaves of *G. psilostemon*, or the yellow leaves of *G.* 'Ann Folkard'.

Other wild geraniums that are mostly evergreen are: *G. macrorrhizum*, *G.* × *oxonianum*, *G. phaeum*, *G.* × *monacense*, *G. reflexum*, *G. pulchrum*, *G. pyrenaicum*, *G. robustum*, *G. versicolor*, *G. traversii* and hybrids.

The leaves are generally rounded, but this is frequently lost in the divisions and subdivisions that occur. The names reflect the leaf divisions, such as cut-leafed geranium, or *G. dissectum*. A rare example with a simple rounded leaf, rather like a pelargonium, is *G. potentilloides*, but this is an exception. Most leaves are divided into five divisions, the largest in the middle front, a pair at the side front, and a smaller pair at the back. This can be seen in *G. canariense*, or in a more rounded fashion in *G.* × *oxonianum* var. *thurstonianum*. The wild plant, *G. dissectum*, sums up the extreme to which leaf division can reach. The roundedness of the leaf is apparent in *G. pyrenaicum*, or in the round-leaved variety, *G. rotundifolium*, even though the five leaf divisions are still visible.

Spiky leaves are common, and this is taken to extreme in *G. clarkei*. Pointed leaves are also found in *G.* 'Ann Folkard' AGM. The leaves of *G. dalmaticum* and *G. wallichianum* 'Buxton's Blue' are much blunter at the tips of their leaf divisions.

Separating wild geraniums into three groups, small-leaved, medium-leaved and large-leaved types, is a convenient way of separating the natural order in the wild (and the garden); examples of each are *G. renardii*, *G. nodosum* and *G. pratense*.

Leaves are often dark green. Very little variation is apparent within the genus, and variegation is infrequent, seen in a few such as the 'Variegatum' forms of *G. macrorrhizum* and *G. phaeum*. Bluish or glaucous leaves are found in *G. harveyi*, silvery leaves in *G. argenteum* and dark leaves in *G. esclliflorum* and *G. sessiliflorum* 'Nigricans'.

G. 'Salome'
LEFT *This hybrid of G. lambertii and G. procurrens has yellow foliage, which is not widely seen in geraniums.*

G. canariense
BELOW *This attractive fragrant perennial has leaves up to 25 cm (10 in) wide with succulent bases.*

G. esclliflorum 'Nigricans'
ABOVE *Dark foliage contrasts with the small white flowers that cover this ground-hugging plant. Given the right spot it makes a good, compact plant.*

G. pyrenaicum
LEFT *The rounded leaf shape and leaf indentations of this species are quite striking and give this plant a degree of individuality.*

G. Purpureum
ABOVE *These bold leaves are divided into five lobes, each of which are then divided into other lobes at the extremities.*

GERANIUMS IN THE GARDEN

Create smart combinations of geraniums and other plant species. Judicial plantings can provide your garden with some wonderful colour schemes.

One is spoiled with choice when gardening with wild geraniums as border plants. Their natural propensity to form mounds and hummocks can be used to cover open soil (to be avoided at all times) and to suppress weeds. They have to be checked just in case they take over and begin to swamp other plants in the border.

One surprising fact is that there are relatively few wild species geraniums used in gardens. It is certainly less than two percent of all known species, so this points to strong conservatism and sticking to well-known varieties. The herbaceous border is a very conservative place, but it can be made more adventurous if you wish. The time is now ripe for for some experimentation.

There is a hard core of six popular species used predominantly in borders, *G. × magnificum* AGM, *G. endressii* AGM, *G. versicolor*, *G. macrorrhizum*, *G. sanguineum* and *G. himalayense*, of which many hybrids are cultivated.

Many wild geraiums do well at the front of a typical herbaceous border in full sun, such as the Bloody cranesbill, *G. sanguineum*, or its variety, *G. s. lancastrense*. There is something wonderful about growing *G. sanguineum* in the garden, for when it is grown just right it takes on exactly the form and exuberance of a good clump one might find in the wild. In addition the red of Bloody cranesbill is always distinctive wherever one meets it. This is a characteristic that is not always true for other plant species grown from wild stock in the garden. The trailing stems of the prostrate growing *G. wallichianum* from the Himalayas will also do very well at the front of the border, but it should be in a shady part since it will not tolerate full sun. The cultivar 'Buxton's Blue' AGM has rich blue colours and these blues are actually enhanced in shady areas.

Conditions

Those gardening on chalk or limestone will find that both *G. sanguineum* and *G. pratense* perform best since they are found naturally on limestone. Limestone is well drained so these species do not mind drought conditions and they enjoy being in full sun. In contrast, *G. soboliferum* likes to be kept moist while being in full sun. Your own garden conditions (aspect and drainage) will dictate which varieties are best for you.

Shade

Borders in light shade can accommodate most wild geraniums. Semi-shade is perfect for *G. endressii* AGM of which *G. e.* 'Russell Pritchard' is a useful trailer. More shade lovers are *G. wallichianum* and *G. palustre*, although the latter will also grow in open beds. Other wild geraniums for the border include *G. grandiflorum*, especially its dwarf, var. alpinum, *G. ibericum* with its showy flowers, *G. pratense* the largest of Britain's native wild geraniums, and *G. psilostemon*, the Armenian wild geranium. *G. macrorrhizum*, which grows as a compact plant, is also popular.

The flowering periods and times in the border vary according to the species, cultivar and hybrid. There are types to choose that will give a flowering period from early spring to late autumn, but generally wild geraniums flower from late spring to mid summer. Wild geraniums

---

WILD GERANIUMS FOR LIGHT AND SHADE

With their natural adaptation to dappled light, there is a wide variety of wild species geraniums that can be employed in wooded, semi-wooded or shade, and glade gardens. They will succeed in these conditions where it is difficult to get other plants to thrive.

Light shade	Dry shade and wild gardens
G. endressii AGM	G. lucidum
G. gracile	G. macrorrhizum
G. lambertii	G. nodosum
G. macrorrhizum	G. psilostemon
G. nodosum	G. robertianum
G. phaeum	
G. psilostemon	
G. sinense	
G. sylvaticum	
G. versicolor	
G. x oxonianum	

G. 'Sirak'
RIGHT *The pink and cream colours of 'Sirak' and Old Man's Beard (Clematis vitalba) indicate high summer when the air is full of the soporific scents of the clematis. An opportune wand of the clematis trails through the geranium to make this happy association.*

SEASONAL WILD GERANIUMS

A variety of wlld geraniums can provide the gardener with flowers from spring to autumn. Below are some examples of good early- and late-flowering species.

Spring to early summer	Summer to early autumn
G. albiflorum	G. lambertii
G. libani	G. pogonanthum
G. maculatum	G. rubifolium
G. reflexum	G. sinense
G. rivulare	G. thunbergii
G. sylvaticum	G. wallchianum

grown as mounds can be cut back immediately after the initial flowering to stimulate another crop of flowers later on. Asian species tend to flower after mid summer.

For those planning colour schemes for borders, there is great variety from which to choose. Wild geraniums can succeed in whatever colour persuasion you like, for their key feature lies in their ability to provide a spread of colour that is not challenged by any other group of plants. The virtue of gardening with wild geraniums is that they have a natural predisposition to growing in shady areas. The fact that so many wild geraniums are meadow and woodland-edge species gives them a distinct advantage over other garden plants that shy away from shady areas. Many grow to about 1m (3ft) high, making them extremely useful plants.

WILD GERANIUMS BY COLOUR

Use a variety of wild geraniums to complement other species and cultivars in the herbaceous border. Some allowance should be given to amount of space that a mature plant will require after a few years.

Red-purple	White	Blue
G. argentum x cinereum	G. albiflorum	G. erinathum
G. incanum	G. clarkei 'Kashmir White'	G. himalyense
G. kishtvariense	G. macrorrhizum 'Album'	G. libani
G. ocellatum	G. pratense 'Galactic'	G. malviflorum
G. psilostemon	G. richardsonii	G. pratense
G. stapfianum	G. robertianum 'Album'	G. platypetalum

Wild geraniums make beautiful feature plants, but they can also be combined with other plants to make a really stunning show. *G.* 'Ann Folkard' AGM is an excellent mixer and will make a wonderful contribution to any herbaceous border. It is a vigorous and spreading plant that is relatively easy to grow and its colours may be enhanced by planting it with the silver grey foliage of *Artemisia* 'Powis Castle' AGM. Astilbes are also a good foil with their various shades of pink to deep red. 'Ann Folkard' AGM is a sterile hybrid that has to be propagated from its own rootstock. It was originally raised by the Reverend O.G. Folkard in 1973 at his nursery in Lincolnshire, England, and has proved popular with gardeners ever since.

G. versicolor
ABOVE *The small white flowers have notched petals and are borne on a straggling stem. It grows well in the shade of a woodland or wild garden.*

G. sylvaticum 'Mayflower' AGM
LEFT *Growing in the dappled shade at the edge of a woodland these spring bloomers contribute generously to the garden structure.*

G. 'Ann Folkard' AGM
OPPOSITE *This cultivar has an open growth pattern and the young leaves are blotched with yellow. It can be grown through a variety of other plants, such as here with Artemisia 'Powis Castle' AGM.*

G. ibericum subsp. jubatum
LEFT *Subtle differences from the normal form are seen in this subspecies: heavier veining, bluer petals, more hair on the buds and stems, and the flowers are smaller.*

ALPINES, SCREES AND TROUGHS

Many of the world's wild geraniums occur naturally in what are known as 'alpine regions', which are defined as all areas more than 1000m (3,281 feet) above sea-level. This is not a vast height, and therefore this habitat encompasses most of the mountain ranges of the world. The eastern, central and western European mountains, including the Alps and the Pyrenees are very important areas for wild geraniums.

Scree gardens
To create a scree garden that is ideal for wild geraniums, the soil should be very porous. Grit, chippings and small rocks, such as tufa, provide lots of pits and holes for seeds and seedlings to grow in. The site should be hot, receiving as much sun as possible, and preferably raised towards the sun. Typically, *G. malviflorum* likes very poor-quality soil in full sun. Other plants to consider for scree beds are *G. stapifianum*, *G. tuberosum*, *G. argentum*, *G. dahuricum*, and *G. farreri*. Rain needs to run off a scree garden immediately so that the ground warms up quickly. Most varieties need watering, but *G. collinum* is drought tolerant and is therefore useful in a dry garden.

Rockeries
Rockeries make wonderful homes for some of the larger species, such as *G. × cantabrigiense* or *G. donianum*, a species that originates in Western China. *G. × lindavicum* 'Apple Blossom' is a very accommodating plant, since it does well wherever it is placed in a rock or alpine garden, scree or trough.

Troughs
If want to replicate the sparse soils of the mountain slopes and screes in a container or trough, choose *G. cinereum*, *G. dalmaticum*, *G. × lindavicum* 'Lissadell', *G. pylzowianum*, and *G. sessiliflorum* subspecies 'Novae-zelandiae' from New Zealand, as its name spells out.

G. macrorrhizum 'Album' AGM
LEFT *Enough space has to be allowed for this large plant since it produces a myriad of these peculiar shaped flowers. The stamens are twice as long as the petals. The flowers are visited by bees, but the foliage is not often attacked by larvae since this perennial is sticky and aromatic.*

GROUND COVER

As hardy perennials, wild geraniums provide abundant green foliage cover when they are not in flower, their mass of leaves contributing valuably to the pleasure of the garden. One of the effects of growing wild geraniums as groundcover is that weeds are suppressed, making for a low-maintenance garden once the plants are properly established.

The way that wild geraniums grow is conducive to their success as groundcover plants. Most geraniums grow in one of two ways: first, as mounds, second, as branched and upstanding plants, and when any of them grow *en masse* they tend to fill the space. Many gardeners grow wild geraniums as single species groundcover plants, or with each other for an attractive show, but you could also devise new combinations with other species.

Some wild geraniums can be used to cover the ground at the front of the traditional stepped herbaceous border, and here they may look fine as showy individual plants. Unicolour mounds of *G. sylvaticum* 'Album' or *G. clarkei* can look very special. Species such as *G. endressi* AGM can also be grown alongside red Lychnis or purple veronicas. If you want groundcover through a temperate winter, use *G. versicolor* or *G. macrorrhizum,* which keep their leaves when the temperature drops.

Wild geraniums perform well in dappled sunlight. This panders to their natural propensity to hug woodland edges and to exploit dappled glades. While *G. macrorrhizum* with its red-stemmed flowers has been used a lot in the past, now many gardeners are seeking a more unusual alternative. Great displays can be created using *G. sylvaticum* or *G. himalayense* with its attractive drifts of soft blue.

Some red geraniums are at their finest in full sun, such as *G. psilostemon* or *G.* 'Patricia'. Cascading from a wall, *G. wallichianum* hybrids can look dramatic in the evening light and can cover 1m² (40in²) of vertical space. An interesting *wallichianum* form, *Thurstonianum*, has bizarre-shaped petals and also does well in full sun.

LEFT *Many perennial geraniums grow well in shady conditions, where their attenuated growth and propensity for blooming in dappled light can be well exploited.*

In larger gardens, drifts of geraniums can give cover and height as tall as Queen Anne's lace (*Anthriscus sylvaticus*), up to 1m (3ft) tall. Some delicately-coloured varieties are at their best here, including *G.* × *oxonianum*, or indeed the white form of Herb Robert.

Groundcover wild geraniums can be useful as a space-filler or weed suppressor in larger gardens. Invasive geraniums include *G. orientalitibeticum* and *G. pylzowianum*. The groundcover that most geraniums provide during the summer persists through much of autumn and winter. This is sometimes enhanced by the foliage turning red when it dies off or when it is stressed by drought. *G. sessiliflorum* has evergreen leaves and the low mounds that the plant makes provide valuable groundcover and visual interest during the winter.

GROUND COVER
Plants for either sun or shade, tallest first

G. × *magnificum* AGM
G. macrorrhizum
G. × *oxonianum*
G. himalayense
G. wlassovianum
G. procurrens
G. × *cantabrigiense*
G. dalmaticum
G. × *riversleaianum*

G × *oxonianum*

G. clarkei
LEFT *Named after the British botanist C.B. Clarke, this species is found to 4,200m (14,000 ft) in the Kashmir mountains. Retaining many of its hardy characteristics this perennial makes a significant contribution to the structure of the typical herbaceous border with its finely-cut leaves and large white flowers and various cultivars.*

G. sylvaticum 'Album'
OPPOSITE *Growing as a typical woodland species with long stems and rather open growth, this white-flowered wood cranesbill is just the choice for areas under trees or alongside hedgerows, in an orchard or in any wild garden.*

G. kishtvariense
ABOVE *Native to Kashmir and with its name reflecting the district in which it was originally collected, Kishtwar, this species was introduced by the British botanist, Roy Lancaster.*

G. renardii
ABOVE *Named after Russian naturalist K.I. Renard, it has white flowers with wedge-shaped, notched petals and fine dark veins. It is native to rock cliffs of the Caucasus mountains of Europe and is suitable for growing in rock gardens and scree beds.*

GERANIUMS BY GROUP

THERE ARE MANY wild geranium species of Western Europe that are not cultivated in gardens, yet they adorn waysides and woodlands, as well as urban wastelands. Some are small, weedy and annual, while others that are larger, more striking and perennial have been specially selected for the garden. With such a wide variety of species, there are cranesbills that naturally fall into groups and many others that have their own single attributes. Understanding these groups will help you choose the right plants for your own garden.

G. dissectum
ABOVE *This wild species from Europe has the tiniest flowers set among filigree foliage.*

G. riversleaianum 'Mavis Simpson'
RIGHT *Creating a mass of flowers, it can be used for effective groundcover in a border or rock garden for it is an effective trailing plant.*

SANGUINEUM GROUP

This widespread and attractive group provides some of the most striking and popular wild geraniums for the garden. Whether adorning the wayside in their natural habitat or carefully cultivated in a border, these plants add welcome colour.

THE MOST IMPORTANT wild geranium in the garden is *G. sanguineum*, the Bloody Cranesbill, a familiar species for formal gardens with traditional herbaceous borders. Gardeners with a more informal attitude, which may be embraced with the term 'wild gardening' or 'wildflower gardening', have employed the services of wild native species such as *G. pratense*, *G. sylvaticum* and *G. phaeum* (meadow, wood and dusky cranesbills respectively.) Native species reward time and effort with interesting foliage and colour.

Bloody Cranesbill (Sanguineum)

One of the finest native geraniums of Europe is the Bloody Cranesbill, *G. sanguineum*, that is named specifically after the bloody colour of its petals. It is always a thrill to see this growing in the wild, whether it is in a cluster of wild flowers in Central Massif, France, or on a coastal limestone outcrop overlooking the Atlantic Ocean in the Burren, western Ireland. Widespread throughout Europe this species is found right through to Asia, and it is easily grown in gardens of North America too. Its brilliance is always to be applauded for it seems to do well in austere conditions – often rocky, hot and dry. It does not mind a considerable amount of frost. In the garden it grows just fine as a hardy perennial. It does have an albino form called *G. sanguineum* 'Album' that has also been accorded AGM status. In the wild it always seems to grow true to type and I have never seen an albino flower – although such an occurrence in the wild is possible in just about all genera of plants and presumably was the origin of this white form.

G. sanguineum
ABOVE LEFT *The true species Bloody Cranesbill has the most brilliant colours. It forms mounds of vegetation and remains in flower for about a month.*

G. sanguineum var. striatum AGM
LEFT *Originally known as G. s. var. lancastriense, these delicate flowers have typical pink veining along their petals.*

G. sanguineum 'Shepherd's Warning' AGM
ABOVE *Flowers are a deep pink and the plants are a little more compact compared to the species.*

G. sanguineum 'Album'
OPPOSITE *The white cultivar of the Bloody Cranesbill is similar to many white forms of other species but it can be identified by its telltale divided leaves.*

Bloody Cranesbill can also be grown in the garden in one of its many other forms, of which there are about forty available from nurseries. Of note are *G. sanguineum* 'Shepherd's Warning' AGM and *G. sanguineum* 'Nyewood', which is a magenta red. *G. sanguineum* var. 'Striatum' AGM is named after the purple veins on its white petals – a sort of purple-veined white Bloody Cranesbill. There is a dark-leaved Bloody Cranesbill available called *G. sanguineum* 'Nigricans'.

G. Robertianum

Herb Robert (*G. robertianum*) is an annual weed that has attracted more attention in the past for its medicinal qualities (for curing all sorts of internal and external complaints) than for its contribution to gardening. It is, however, a beautiful plant with pinnate leaflets and tiny pink flowers. Its place in the garden may well be opportunistic since it can occur as an annual weed that can then be nurtured; a good place for it is in a crevice on a brick wall alongside Ivy-leaved toadflax, *Cymbalaria muralis*. The downside of Herb Robert is that the leaves have an unpleasant smell. There is also a smaller version of Herb Robert, called Little Robert, *G. purpureum*, but this is rare in the wild and is not much grown in gardens.

Albino forms of Herb Robert occur quite naturally in the wild, and some of these have been cultivated for the garden. These white Herb Roberts include 'Celtic White' and 'Cygnus', which lack red pigmentation in their stems and leaves, and 'Album', which is a trailing plant.

Individual plants can grow up to 61cm (2 ft) if supported. They are green in summer and patchy red in autumn giving rise to its old name, Dragon's blood. The species is found throughout Europe, Asia, North Africa and North America.

Another small wild geranium likely to be seen along the wayside is *G. dissectum*, the Cut-leaved Cranesbill. The leaves are very attractive and when grown in a wild-flower mix in a patch of grass, such as in an orchard, makes the grass much more interesting. This species, like many of the wild geraniums, is more for the enthusiast and collector than weekend gardeners.

North America

In North America there are not as many wild geraniums as in Europe, and some European species have naturalized there. Among the natives are *G. maculatum* (the Wild Geranium), *G. bicknellii* (Bicknell's Cranesbill) and *G. carolinianum* (Carolina Geranium, or Small-flowered Cranesbill). Richardson's Geranium (*G. richardsonii*) is a species found in light woods and woodland edges, while *G. viscosissimum* (the Sticky Geranium, on account of its sticky leaves) makes an attractive border plant in full sun (in Europe and North America), although in some east coast gardens it can become a lawn weed.

G. sanguineum 'Nyewood'
ABOVE *The vibrant magenta of these delicate flowers makes this a popular form of the Bloody Cranesbill.*

G. robertianum
LEFT *Although often ignored by gardeners, these beautiful flowers would look wonderful in tiny crevices.*

G. × *oxonianum*
OPPOSITE *This is a hybrid formed from* G. versicolor *and* G. endressii, *the* 'oxonianum' *indicating that it originated in Oxford.*

ENDRESSII AND OXONIANUMS

Geranium endressii AGM is a particularly stunning geranium for any border. It has its own scrumptious shade of pink that fades a little, and its petals are slightly reflexed. There is a distinctive notch on the end of each petal. *G. endressii* AGM is a native of the alpine parts of the Pyrenees mountains, occurring mostly on the French side of the mountains rather than in Spain, where it lives in wet meadows and on streambanks. In the garden it provides exuberant growth and is ideal for groundcover, being cut back to ground level at the end of flowering. There are just a few cultivars of *G. endressii* AGM including white, dark and rose named cultivars, as well as *G. e.* 'Wargrave Pink' that has salmon-pink flowers. Where *G. endressii* AGM has been crossed with *G. versicolor* the resultant hybrid has been marketed as *G. × oxonianum*.

G. × oxonianum is a very vigorous plant for the herbaceous border or shady area under the trees, for this hybrid has rid itself of the mounded habit of *G. endressii* AGM to become a 1m (3ft) tall plant with small, soft pink flowers as dainty as *G. versicolor*. Among the interesting cultivars are *G × o.* 'Wargrave Pink' AGM with greater pinkness in its petals, 'Old Rose' which is more of a mauve pink, and 'Hollywood' which has small flowers of variable white and pink. Another important product of this union, is *G. × o.* 'A. T. Johnson' which is silvery-pink. *G × o.* 'Thurstonianum' has very narrow petals that have not developed properly such that the overall effect of the little flowers is to indicate a very dark purple because the dark veins on the petals have been forced together. As a specimen it does well in full sun and makes a worthwhile contribution to the border, and it always gets a second glance.

G. endressii AGM has been crossed with another species cranesbill, *G. traversii* – a rose- or white-flowered native of the Chatham Islands in New Zealand. This has produced *G. × riversleaianum* of which two important cultivars are in widespread use in gardens. These are '*G × r.* 'Mavis Simpson' with silvery shell-pink flowers, and *G. × r.* 'Russell Prichard' AGM which has trailing stems with magenta pink flowers.

G. × *oxonianum* 'Wargrave Pink' AGM
ABOVE *Grouped as a salmon-pink-flowered cultivar, this herbaceous perennial is, according to its accolade of AGM, hardy throughout the whole of the British Isles. It is therefore hardy through most of the seaboards of North America. Once known as* G. endressii *'Wargrave Pink'.*

G. × *oxonianum* 'Lace Time'
RIGHT *Named after its lace-like veins, that look just like the tiny veins on a butterfly's wing, this dainty cultivar can be identified by its distinctive notched petals.*

G. × oxonianum 'Summer Surprise'
LEFT *These soft but rich pink flowers are attractive. At their base the pink gives way to a small area of creamy green, from which the pale flowering parts arise.*

G. × oxonianum 'Thurstonianum'
ABOVE AND RIGHT *Weird and wonderful flowers are produced by this aberrant cultivar. The petals are short, widely separated, strap-like and the veins are bunched, making the flower look very dark. This is very variable in flower colour, and can produce semi-double flowers in the spring, since some stamens become petaloid, but it is consistent in its growth habit, being tall and bushy. While the flowers are of keen interest close-up, the large plants fill up large swathes of space in sunny borders and reward the gardener with lavish purple flowers from spring to the autumn.*

WOOD GERANIUMS

Bridging the gap between the countryside flora and the herbaceous border the wood geraniums and their cultivars come with a hardiness factor that is useful in everyday gardening.

THERE ARE SIX species from Europe and Asia that are put into this group on the basis that they all have large, broad lobed leaves and upright flowers; they are *G. sylvaticum, G. rivulare, G. pseudosibiricum, G. albiflorum, G. psilostemon* and *P. procurrens*. Here are two of the species that are most commonly found in gardens.

G. sylvaticum

The Wood Cranesbill, *G. sylvaticum*, in its natural haunts in woods, meadows and open stony ground, has upright flowers of reddish-mauve or pink. It has a distinctive flower and the plant may be found to 2,400 m (8000 ft),

occurring throughout Europe, from Scotland and England across to Asia. In the garden it will do well both in shade and in full sun. In some places in England it is scattered along roadside verges where it makes a welcome addition to the flora.

With natural adaptations for a shady garden, or dappled light by a fence or wood margin, this species would do well in scree and pebble gardens as well. When the plant is grown underneath other plants so that the flowers protrude above, some interesting colour mixes and combinations can be produced.

The attractive characteristic of *G. sylvaticum* is the light centre to the flowers, and this can be seen also

G. sylvaticum
LEFT *Tall and handsome, this plant is reliable for borders and banks in and out of shade. There are many forms and cultivars, including two AGM plants, 'Album' and 'Mayflower'.*

G. psilostemon AGM
RIGHT *This perennial is hardy through the whole of the British Isles, and most of the seaboards of North America. 'Bressingham Flair' and 'Gold Leaf' are examples of cultivars.*

in some of its pretty hybrids and clones such as *G. s.* 'Mayflower' AGM in purple-blue, and *G. sylvaticum* 'Silva' in magenta-blue. There are at least fourteen forms, subspecies, clones, varieties and cultivars of the Wood Cranesbill available from nurseries, including one other plant that has been awarded the prestigious AGM, *G. sylvaticum* 'Album'.

Geranium psilostemon

Next to the Bloody Cranesbill, the most strident of the cranesbill reds is *G. psilostemon*. This was originally called *G. armenum* which describes its native haunt, Armenia in Eastern Europe. The large flowers have a magnificent black centre from which black veins radiate. A superb mixer in the border, since red will go with just about anything, especially if it is hot, the species has been used a great deal to produce other hybrids through mixing of its genes.

Losing hardly any of the appeal of the flower, *G.* 'Patricia' was produced from a combination of *G. psilostemon* with *G. endressi*, a pink species native to the Pyrenees mountains of Southern Europe. Another hybridization was between *G. psilostemon* and *G. procurrens*, a native of the Himalayas with purple flowers and black centres. All these parents and hybrids have attractive dark centres to the flowers.

A GERANIUM HYBRID

This is how a hybrid is produced. Taking two distinct species and crossing them produces a hybrid that combines the characteristics and virtues of the two parents.

G. psilostemon AGM
Bright petals and dark eye

G. procurrens
Small but bright flowers

G. 'Ann Folkard' AGM
Large flowers with a bright eye and contrasting foliage.

MEADOW CRANESBILLS

Meadow Cranesbills bring a wonderful wild, untamed look to a garden. These perennials will bring a splash of colour year after year and can be grown in various conditions around the garden.

THERE ARE A NUMBER of important garden species belonging to the Meadow Cranesbill (*Pratense*) group; these include *G. pratense* itself with all its varieties, *G. himalayense* and *G. clarkei*. Their common characteristics are that they are all perennials with large blue or pink flowers usually exhibiting glandular hairs. The Meadow Cranesbill, *G. pratense*, has the distinction of occurring in the wild from Western Europe to Western China. Both *G. pratense* and *G. himalayense* make important contributions to gardens in North America where they have been introduced. Growing particularly on limestone in its natural habitat, fortunately *G. pratense* does not keep to this requirement in the garden where it can be grown without too much difficulty as a meadow mix.

There are other wild geraniums that have already adapted to life in full sun away from their natural habitat of the woodland edge, and these include the Marsh Cranesbill (*G. palustre*) and the Dusky Cranesbill (*G. phaeum*).

These two wild geraniums can be grown in wet gardens or around ponds since in the wild they occur in damp meadows.

Anyone contemplating a wild meadow should not exclude *G. pratense*. This is a species native to parts of Europe through to Asia. In some parts of the world it has naturalized along roadside verges and is quite at home in long grass, raising its flowering heads among the vegetation in various shades of violet blue, pale blue, pink and white.

There are probably more cultivars of this species than of any other wild geranium species (there are 38 listed), indicating its importance in gardening. The various coloured flowers available are reflected in the variety of cultivars, such as 'Silver Queen', 'Blue Chip', *f. albiflorum* and 'Rose Queen'. Two very interesting and attractive cultivars that are well worth growing are *G. p.* 'Plenum Caeruleum', which has double flowers in mauve-pink, and 'Mrs Kendall Clark' AGM whose light blue petals are strongly veined in a ghostly, almost ethereal, slate white.

G. pratense 'Plenum Caeruleum' LEFT *Double flowers like this are even more interesting since they tend not to look like the normal form, and it was this sort of quirk of nature that led the Victorian gardeners to go for something different. This is an old-fashioned wild geranium that grows well in the border.*

G. pratense

RIGHT *There is something plain and simple in a wild geranium flower that makes it very appealing. The five petals and the uncluttered reproductive parts are shown at their best and most uniform in this Meadow Cranesbill.*

SELECTED VARIETIES OF DUSKY CRANESBILL

G. p. 'Album'	pure white
G. p. 'Blue Shadow'	blue
G. p. 'Calligrapher'	blue-purple to deep violet
G. p. 'Joan Baker'	red-purple
G. p. var. lividus	blue-purple
G. p. 'Langthorn's Blue'	blue-purple
G. p. 'Lily Lovell'	deep mauve
G. p. 'Mourning Widow'	purple-black
G. p. 'Pink Spice'	pink
G. p. 'Rose Madder'	brown-pink

G. himalayense 'Gravetye' AGM

LEFT *Named after the house, Gravetye Manor in Sussex, England, where the father of wildflower gardening, William Robinson lived, this cultivar is characterized by the suffusion of red towards the base of the petals. It was awarded its AGM since it is a hardy perennial throughout the British Isles, and that stands it in good stead for gardening in many areas of North America.*

GERANIUM PALMATUM

The impressive size of the Palmatum group means that they are bound to make a statement wherever they are planted. To make the most of these magnificent plants, allow them the space their stature deserves.

TWO WILD SPECIES GERANIUMS from Madeira are in the Palmatum group because of their rosette of leaves and large size. These magnificent species are *P. palmatum* and *G. maderense*. They are short-lived perennials, growing outside in Mediterranean climates, or in large greenhouses and conservatories. *G. palmatum* was once called *G. anemonifolium*, because of its anemone-shaped leaves, and it has retained the name connection as it belongs in the *Anemonifolia* section.

Not far removed from the Palmatum group is another large-growing geranium called *G. canariense* and this shares with the familiar Herb Robert and *G. rubescens* exclusive membership in the Robertianum group because of the similarity of leaf shape. They are the largest species in Western Europe.

These three spectacular wild geraniums are from some of the westerly outposts of Europe, and make superb subjects in gardens today. As they are all from relatively the same place on the globe, they might as well be called the Giant Atlantic Cranesbills to distinguish them from much smaller wild geraniums.

They are all native to the islands: *G. canariense* comes from the Canaries, *G. maderense* AGM and *G. palmatum* are both from Madeira. All are distinctive plants that

G. canariense
ABOVE *Native to Tenerife and other islands within the Canary Isles, this is a fine-looking species that grows as a rosette of leaves and flowers, just like it near neighbor,* G. maderense.

G. palmatum
LEFT *Native to Madeira, this popular perennial species is often grown in gardens or conservatories because of its large size.*

can grow up to 1m (3ft) tall, and the first two have a big rosette of basal leaves that makes them very distinctive. Their flowers are a soft pink to purple and are borne on tall compound umbels. A mature specimen takes up a lot of space and becomes a focus of attention and has many attributes as an architectural plant.

It is fascinating to see *G. maderense* growing roadside and in disturbed areas such as picnic areas in Madeira. The species is under threat in Madeira since it is endemic to the island. Fortunately it is widely grown elsewhere, and therefore gardeners are providing a valuable service in keeping this, and other endangered species going.

The landscape of these Atlantic Ocean islands is volcanic, rugged and windswept, and it is clear why these wild geraniums are so large and sturdy since they have adapted to these extreme conditions. These varieties are not suitable for a small garden, but to bulk up a large herbaceous border or for a spectacular specimen in a large pot they are ideal.

Madeira
LEFT *The isolation of the Madeira volcanic islands in the Western Atlantic has promoted the evolution of a large number of endemic species including wild geraniums. There is ample habitat for* G. maderense *to prosper in the mild weather.*

G. maderense
LEFT *This is a superlative species, being the largest known wild geranium with the largest leaves. It will grow to 1.5m (5 ft) tall and its leaves are 60cm (2 ft) wide. It is best in Mediterranean climates and should be grown in a greenhouse in places with cool winters. It is space hungry, so not for regular garden greenhouses. In hotter climates and in spacious gardens it has a great presence.*

DUSKY CRANESBILLS

The group described as 'Dusky Cranesbills' is also described as the 'phaeum group'. Suitable for planting in tall borders or as part of a meadow or wild garden, this group has much to offer the gardener.

This group of three species, *G. phaeum*, *G. reflexum* and *G. aristatum*, grows as tall branching plants with nodding flowers and reflexed or widely-spreading petals. All three are cultivated in gardens; *G. phaeum* is the most popular; *G. aristatum* is a hummocky plant with hairy greyish-green leaves from the mountains of South Albania; and *G. reflexum* is ideal as groundcover with its nodding rosy flowers.

There is an ecclesiastical connection with *G. phaeum*, the Dusky Cranesbill. The dark, dramatic colours of the flowers have engendered thoughts of mourning, thus it is also called the 'Mourning Widow' and is often marketed as that cultivar. As an upright plant which shows off its tall dark flowers at the level of the long grass that you might find growing around a cemetery, it is perhaps not incidental that this species is frequently found around old churchyards in England, even in the centre of a large city like London. Gardeners seeking to include this remarkable species in a dark border, or to have it naturalized in a wild meadow, orchard or along a woodland walk, will find this a most accommodating species. There are even more varieties of the Dusky Cranesbill to enthuse over than the Wood Geraniums, indeed there are over 30 varieties, and of these at least seven are attractive dark forms, such as the dramatic *G. phaeum* 'Lily Lovell'.

LEFT *There are about 30 varieties of the Dusky Cranesbill and many of them have emphasized the intriguing dark colors of the petals. Among these are 'Calligrapher', 'Lily Lovell' and 'Mourning Widow'.*

RIGHT *A dusky appearance can be used to great effect as one might display other chocolate or dark-coloured flowers, such as chocolate Cosmos, in a border.*

PELARGONIUMS

T HE WORLD OF PELARGONIUMS is far bigger than the relatively neat world of perennial geraniums or cranesbills. There has been much more hybridization and selection for colour of leaf or colour and shape of the flowers. The flowers are larger in pelargoniums than in perennial geraniums, and the variety of groups within the pelargoniums is also much greater. There are plenty of species pelargoniums about which to enthuse, and there are also plenty of small groups that have considerable followings, such as the ever-popular angels.

P. 'Highfields Flair'
ABOVE *Bright colours and large trusses of flowers typify the Highfields range of zonal pelargoniums.*

P. splendide
LEFT *This primary hybrid pelargonium is often mistaken for the species pelargonium P. 'Tricolor', which is very similar but has narrower leaves.*

INTRODUCTION

Pelargoniums have been so widely crossed and selected by gardeners and plantsmen over the centuries that many thousands of types have been selected, many of which have been lost to history. The enthusiasm and energy to select has, however, hardly waned.

PELARGONIUMS CAN BE recognized in flower engravings from the early seventeenth century, although they would then have been referred to as geraniums. Engravings of the garden of Henry IV of France in 1608 show pelargoniums used alongside plants such as crown imperial fritillaries (*Fritillaria imperialis*). Nearly 400 years later the popularity of pelargoniums is just as strong.

Formal gardens, especially French, German and Italian, still use pelargoniums to make bold colour statements. The use of massed ranks of pelargoniums as carpet bedding is popular in parks as well as in formal gardens.

In the vaults of the Linnean Society in London there are 103 herbarium specimens of 'geraniums' collected by Carl Linneaus. Linneaus was the eighteenth-century Swedish naturalist who devised the Binominal System of Nomenclature, the recognized international language for botanists, scientists and gardeners. Linneaus' 'geraniums' were in fact a mixture of species of the *Pelargonium*, *Geranium* and *Erodium* genera.

Pelargoniums were originally spread around the globe by seafarers. They proved popular because they were easy to keep alive as a result of their succulent nature. Eighteenth-century emigrants to Australia took pelargoniums with them. Earlier, Captain Cook found native geraniums at Botany Bay in 1770 – *G. pilosum* (now *G. solanderi*) and *Pelargonium australe*. Australian settlers found that pelargoniums grew vigorously and could be grown in dense hedgerows. Today, in Australia, pelargoniums are still grown in hedgerows or as blanket cover cascading down walls. This effect can only be created in

P. 'L'Elégante'
LEFT *An old-fashioned ivy-leaved pelargonium with interesting leaves and pale purple-pink flowers, this does well in pots on patios.*

P. iconicum
LEFT *This is the
Figured Stork's
Bill, as featured
by Robert Sweet
in his masterly
1820's volumes
on geraniums.*

Mediterranean climates and some stunning examples of this kind of use can be seen in the Italian Riviera garden, La Mortola (also known as the Hanbury Garden).

It is thought that the seeds of *P. capitatum* initially arrived in Australia from South Africa clinging to sheep's wool. Left-over pieces of carded wool with debris knotted into them were often cast aside, and this has resulted in the dispersal of hundreds of species, not just pelargoniums, in distant lands. Zonal geraniums have done well in Australia since they thrive in a hot climate and do not require constant watering.

Classification

The genus Pelargonium is now made up of 14 sections. Classification is still developing and new sections can be expected in the future. From the point of view of the amateur grower, all the sections are pelargoniums, regardless of their names. In this book we have adopted the traditional way of dealing with pelargonium classification: from the species through the scented pelargoniums, zonals, regals and so on.

Cultivars and Series

Thousands of pelargoniums have been bred.

Between 1860 and 1900, over 9,000 cultivars were produced, and more are being created by the nurseries that busy themselves with pelargonium propagation today. Sadly, the plethora of new breeds has inevitably resulted in the tragic loss of many old pelargonium cultivars, a situation which has been seen across the horticultural spectrum. Series are not always perpetuated by those growers that follow on. The popularity of certain cultivars waxes and wanes as fashions change, they become lost and suddenly a particular cultivar is no longer available.

Series are named after the individuals that created them, or even places and sometimes after rivers. The Deacons series have an ecclesiastical connection. The newer cultivar names are less magical as they are now addressed according to their trade names, which are registered trademarks from commercial companies. Commerical names can be confusing as there may be three names for the plant: the plant breeder's right name, a marketing name and an original nominated name for registration.

Names cannot be reproduced and sold on to anyone unless they have a licence to propagate. However, it is so easy to select new cultivars that amazing selections will be created, whether they are registered or not, while commercial producers will continue to create many new strains.

Enthusiasts can be excused for becoming engrossed in one particular group of pelargoniums, for there are so many groups from which to choose. A pelargonium fan may have a passion for angels simply because of their great charm and light petal colours, or be enthralled by the stalwart zonals that have captivated gardeners for more

CLASSIFICATION

Pelargonium classification has recently been revised and the genus Pelargonium is now thought to be made up of 14 sections. These are listed below, along with their key characteristics and some noteworthy examples.

Section	Characteristics (simplified)	Notes and examples
Campia	low-growers, tufted or rosette habit	Known from a range of species pelargoniums such as P. ovale, P. tricolor and P. elegans.
Ciconium	large plants, lower three petals larger than upper two	Contains many species, including P. peltatum from which ivy-leaved pelargoniums have arisen. Also contains P. zonale.
Cortusina	semi-succulent stems	Known from a few species pelargoniums, typically P. crassicaule that has thick stems.
Glaucophyllum	bluish or gray leaves as glaucous suggests shrubs or subshrubs	A small number of species with a diverse range of leaf shapes, such as lance-shaped (P. lanceolatum) or into three (P. ternate). others with large flowers (P. grandiflorum).
Hoarea	stemless, leaves die as flowers flourish, tubers	Over 70 species including P. longifolium (with long leaves) and P. pinnatum (with pinnate leaves).
Isopetalum	a succulent with white flowers	Known from a single species, P. cotyledonis, meaning the leaves look like cotyledons.
Jenkinsonia	palmatum leaves, large upper petals on an irregular-shaped flower	Includes two species which are hardy in the UK through the winter and are the only two which can survive winters outdoors (except in the worst regions) P. endlicherianum and P. quercetorum – the latter is found in the oak woods of northern Iraq and south east Turkey
Ligularia	No firm characteristsics highly variable	This group may be split into three more sections as there are so many variable as it is so far classified Typical examples are P. rodneyanum and P. fulgidum.
Myrrhidium	pinnate leaves, large upper petals	In the wild members of this group are sprawling weeds and colonists on exposed ground. In hanging baskets some of them prosper since they have a trailing habit. P. multicaule and P. candicans are typical
Otidia	succulent with white flowers	Known from only a small number of species such as P. alternans and P. carnosum .
Pelargonium species	aromatic shrubs or subshrubs, large upper petals	24 species known, including the parents of the scented-leaved, angels, Uniques and regals. Includes P. capitatum
Peristera	annual or perennial, small flowers	Another section named in 1824 by De Candolle from Montpellier. It includes such species as P. australe. 'Peristera' is the Latin word for 'dove', which reflects its leaf shape.
Polycatium	tuberous plants, night-scented flowers	A range of species of which P. triste and P. bowkeri are connoisseur's plants, the former for its subtle scents after dark, and the second for its two types of leaves on the same plant.
Reniformia	Irregular flowers, stems with stipules and petioles	A wide range of species that are aromatic and are well known such as P. fragrans and P. odoratissumum.

than a century with their bright red flowers. In today's world it is easy to be led by the growers who propagate millions of just a few well proven cultivars, but it is a shame to limit yourself to popular tastes. You can branch out and start to collect different groups of pelargoniums for your own interest. It is easy to see how enthusiasts fall for the charms of stellars and cacti pelargoniums, for instance. Their attractive petals are divided in an interesting and unusual starburst effect, giving you a wonderfully showy plant.

You don't need lots of space or a great deal of leisure time to grow pelargoniums successfully. Those busy people who fit gardening in when they can and in restricted spaces can become accomplished growers and derive a great deal of pleasure from these plants.

There are so many varieties to experiment with and colour combinations to develop that are ideal for even the smallest gardens. This includes the dwarfs, minis and micro-minis, which provide an amazing variety of choices. If you want to use perfume to add another dimension to your garden, there are varieties with all manner of scents, enough to fill many enthusiasts' gardens many times over. I acquired a second-hand copy of Derek Clifford's classic 1958 book *Pelargoniums, including the popular 'Geranium'*, complete with the attendant smell of pelargoniums. The book was indelibly infused with the highly characteristic scent thanks to someone having taken cut stems to the book for identification. Every time I consult the book, even in mid-winter, I am reminded of pelargoniums by their scent wafting up with the turn of every page.

The importance of pelargonium scent is manifold. It has contributed to the success of the group around the world, for it is an effective insect deterrent (a few leaves of the scented pelargonium on a table at dinner time will effectively repel flies) and has allowed the plant to survive naturally in the wild in some inhospitable and hostile environments. If you are looking for sheer splendour, some of the showy regals compete with begonias in their floral magnificence.

However, whatever the virtues of particular varieties, gardeners will always have their personal favorites. Stalwarts such as 'Lord Bute' AGM remain popular since they are reliable performers. As with other popular genera, such as *Clematis* or *Rosa*, new varieties come and go all

---

SERIES – ANCIENT AND MODERN
Named by Robert Sweet in the 1820s following his own classification and spelling.

American First Lady	a general series named after American first ladies
Bold	a series of zonals raised by John Gibbons (UK)
Brookside Varieties	raised by Geoff Hopkins (UK)
Bruant types	old varieties named after Bruant of Poitier (France)
Carefree	a commercial series in Europe and N Americal
Cobham Collection	raised by H F Parrett of Cobham, Kent (UK)
Deacons	dwarf cultivars raised by the Reverend Stringer (UK)
Double Dips	selections of zonals with double flowers
Eclipse	a commercial series of late 20th century Holland
Fiat	a commercial series raised by Bruant in France
Flash	a commercial series from N America (not listed in UK)
Harlequin	a series from grafted 'Rouletta' and 'Rivers' series
Hartsook Unique	Modern hybrids with wonderful flowers bred by Francis Hartsook, California (USA) from old UK plants.
Hazel	Dennis Fielding raised this series of Regals named after an area of Manchester, UK, where he lived at the time.
Highfields	a series of zonal cultivars bred by Ken Gamble (UK)
Irenes	also called 'American Irenes', Behringer (USA)
Langley-Smith hybrids	old term for some angels raised by Langley-Smith
Lilliputian zonal series	lost minis of the mid nineteenth century, Fairy and Saxony
Maiden	series raised by Oglevee (USA)
Merite	trademark of Merite Breeding in Wageningen (Holland)
Mosaic Ivy Leaf	Grafted series of trailing pelargoniums with mosaic veining in the foliage.
Norfolk Dwarfs	dwarfs raised by F G Read Norfolk (UK)
Novelty Varieties	these include Cactus, Stellars and Startel cultivars
Occold	a series raised by Reverend Stringer of Occold(UK)
Unique	Series of old scented-leaf pelargoniums with a particular pungent aroma to the foliage (UK).

---

the time. While not all of these new plants are destined to become garden favourites, some will endure and it is well worth being aware of new any varieties that become available. You may find just what you are looking for to complete your own collection.

Gardening with pelargoniums is fun and, more importantly, it is easy. All you need to grow pelargoniums outdoors is lots of strong sunshine and water. As long as you provide your plants with these basic requirements, the insects will generally not bother the progress of pelargoniums. They can be enjoyed indoors and in conservatories as well, but the scents are not so effective indoors and the plants can be more prone to problems from insect pests. In cold climates pelargoniums are treated as annuals as they do not survive the winter, but they are still worth growing for their colour, foliage, and scent. Cuttings are taken in summer or they can be grown from seed, but only true species seed will guarantee a resemblance to the parent plant.

PELARGONIUMS FOR THE PLACE

*Pelargoniums thrive in containers of all kinds, making them one of the most versatile
and easy to place plants in the garden. You can use single specimens for a really striking statement,
or plant swathes of them for a dramatic effect.*

STEPS AND WALLS are ideal places to display pelargoniums. Heat radiated by brickwork increases their growth rate and extends the growing time of the plants. The impact of the blooms is influenced by the colour of the stone, brickwork or paving against which they are placed. Orange flowers look wonderful set against honey-coloured stone, while pink complements the pink stucco of Mediterranean villas. Use bright red flowers to contrast with white walls or place them against dark woodwork for a warmer effect.

In the areas around the Mediterranean, it is not uncommon to find all steps, ledges and windowsills filled with pelargoniums. Bright blooms jostle for space, burst out of grilles or cascade from baskets.

These banks of colour soften the barrier between the garden and the house. In homes without gardens, potted plants add a splash of colour.

Pelargoniums look wonderful in massed ranks in huge jardinières or a single specimen can be placed on a patio or at the water's edge. They can be combined with *Helichrysum petiolare* whose whitish-blue or yellow leaves are good matches. Dark-leaved varieties combine well with *Phormium* sp. or *Ophiopogon planiscapus* 'Nigrescens' AGM.

LEFT *Single plants can be very effective in wall pots, but they have to be watered daily to maintain the desired effect.*

RIGHT *In the absence of searing heat, partial shade for pelargoniums provides great colour and requires less watering.*

LEFT *Potted pelargoniums in different colours can be displayed on ledges, window sills and steps.*

P. 'Rouletta'
LEFT *A red-pink combination is achieved with this marvellous 'Rouletta' that is just as accustomed to climbing as trailing, and is here grown with roses, Maltese Cross (Lychnis coronaria) and pink oxalis.*

P. 'Bright Red Cascade'
ABOVE *This ivy-leaved pelargonium is a ball of tumbling scarlet, as its name suggests.*

P. 'PELFI Diabolo'
ABOVE *Potted 'geraniums' at their most typical are spaced out on steps to add vibrant colour during the summer months. The hotter it gets, the better the display.*

Ivy-leaved pelargoniums look wonderful planted in containers as their neat blooms fall away when they have finished – making them less labour-intensive than plants that need deadheading. Zonal stellars and stellar dwarfs look particularly good in small pots, where they can be combined with smaller plants for maximum visual effect. The whole range of dwarfs and miniatures lend themselves to container display. Dwarf varieties can be planted in tiny pots and containers and displayed on small areas such as windowsills where they can add valuable colour and visual interest. Small pots are portable, so you can move pots around and create a variety of combinations. Garden designer Gertrude Jekyll often used brightly coloured container-grown pelargoniums to enhance a lacklustre border or bed.

Hanging Baskets and Wallpots

Abundant foliage and resplendent flowers in a range of colours make pelargoniums easy to place in a hanging display. There is hardly a form of pelargonium that could not be used in a hanging basket. The exceptions are the very small species, which might be swamped if planted in a basket among other closely packed plants. The ivy-leaved pelargoniums include the cascades – Continentals and Swiss Balconies are all suited for life in hanging baskets and are extremely popular. These can all be bought early or grown from cuttings and then plugged into the basket, after which they make good progress.

The smaller pelargoniums, such as the angels, some of the scented varieties and the miniature ivies can be grown in baskets. If possible place your

P. **'Mini Rose Cascade'**
LEFT *Ivy-leaved pelargoniums, like this one photographed in Slovakia, add brightness to the dark window frame.*

Pelargonium **'Mini Red Cascade' and 'Deacon Birthday'**
BELOW *Window sills and ledges in the Cévennes of France are simply adorned with pelargoniums creating shapes and colours to ponder during a siesta.*

hanging basket at eye level to fully appreciate the colour, form and perfume of your chosen plants.

If you take good care of your hanging basket, it will repay you with a riot of glorious colour. Frequent watering is essential to maintain the plants' good looks (especially as hanging baskets dry out quickly). The advantage of growing pelargoniums in hanging baskets is that they warm up quicker than in the ground, can be moved around to different locations to take advantage of better conditions, and are more likely to stay free from disease.

California boasts some enormous examples of pelargoniums in baskets. This is because the Mediterranean climate of the area allows some of the plants to survive the mild winter. In cooler European winters this is not always possible and new plants will have to be added to the display each year.

P. 'Amethyst'
ABOVE *This double pink pelargonium in the Czech Republic does well on the window sill but still needs to be kept well-watered.*

P. 'Acapulco' and 'Bright Red Cascade'
ABOVE *High in the Mediterranean side of the Massif Central in France at about 1000 m (3,000 ft), the summer is hot enough to support ivy-leaved pelargoniums in a window box, set off by the super-abundance of hydrangeas.*

P. 'Ville de Paris Pink'
ABOVE *Normally sold under this name, this is more formally called P. 'Hederinum'. Its ivy-like leaves are better reflected in its new name. Here, despite its naming, it is superbly set off by being grown in an antique jardinière in rural southern France.*

P. 'Sybil Holmes'
LEFT *Tight clusters of double pink flowers which look just like rose buds is typical of this ivy-leaved cultivar. The balls of pink make spectacular displays.*

PELARGONIUM SPECIES

SPECIES PELARGONIUMS are consistently popular with gardeners around the world. Their undiluted genes mean that these plants are hardy and relatively easy to grow. Like many species plants, they also have the advantage of being little bothered by pests and diseases that can afflict some of the cultivars. There is a species pelargonium for almost any situation in the garden. Whether you require plants for groundcover, shrubs for foliage, or simple flower colour, a species pelargonium could provide the answer. The following pages explain from whence these pelargoniums originate and how to use them to best advantage.

P. stenopetalum
ABOVE *The second Latin name of this South African species translates as 'narrow petals'. Its flower truss is distinctive because of the bright individual flowers.*

Pelargonium rodneyanum
RIGHT *This was originally collected from the wild pasturelands of Australia in 1836. Its rose-pink flowers are borne on an umbel above the plant.*

INTRODUCTION

Species pelargoniums are quite hardy and will provide the garden with a reliable show of colour, form and sometimes scent.

PELARGONIUMS ARE NATURALLY distributed in ten parts of the world. The greatest area of distribution runs several hundred kilometers inland from the coast of Namibia in south west Africa, running south to include most of South Africa, and moving up the east coast of Africa in a broad band, but excluding most of the coast in Mozambique and Somalia. This band runs continuously north to the Gulf of Aden, where, on the north side of the Gulf, there is another area of pelargonium habitat in Yemen, South Yemen and southern Saudi Arabia.

The second largest location for pelargoniums is Australia, stretching across the whole of the southern part of the continent and running several hundred kilometers inland. New Zealand has a large section of suitable habitat on the north of North Island. In addition there are two locations in the South Atlantic that are home to native species of the Pelargonium genus, St. Helena and Tristan da Cunha.

There are three other areas of distribution: a swathe of mountainous countryside linking the Black Sea with the Mediterranean, entirely within Turkey, and an isolated pocket straddling the borders between northern Iraq, eastern Turkey and eastern Iran. The southern tip of Madagascar also supports wild pelargoniums. These areas may have suitable habitats, but many of these habitats are somewhat compromised by man's activities; however, in some mountainous and desert areas much suitable habitat still survives.

About 80 percent of all species occur in the south-western area of South Africa, which is characterized by having only winter rainfall. The amount of rain varies according to the area and elevation but pelargoniums do occur in areas that have as little as 100mm (4in) per year to those with over 750mm (30in) per year. When it is not raining the weather is hot and dry, so this makes South Africa an ideal habitat for succulent pelargoniums.

P. fulgidum
LEFT *A native of South Africa, this species grows near the sea and prefers sandy soil. It can be obtained from nurseries in these two colour forms. It has evergreen leaves and its flowers are borne on umbels well above the plant.*

P. 'Mrs Stapleton'
OPPOSITE *A delight in rich purple with smudges of chocolate, these flowers are generously displayed on long stalks.*

Mediterranean locations

Pelargonium species have also colonized other pockets of Mediterranean climate., but there are two large blocks which have never sported pelargonium species as natives in the wild: these are the coastal Mediterranean countries (except Turkey's coast) and the southern Californian coast. However, some wonderful garden displays can be found in these places, and some introduced pelargoniums have become naturalized on the rocks and in coastal areas.

This section deals with true species described with two Latin names, such as *Pelargonium zonale*, (*P. zonale*). Some varieties are described as species although they do not have two Latin names. Their origins are obscure and their names have acquired various attributes.

Latin names

The second Latin name often describes the species, especially its leaves. For instance *P. zonale*, has zones, or patches, on its leaves, *P. hirstum* has hairless leaves, *P. schizopetalum* has divided leaves, *P. longfolium* has long leaves and *P. coriandrifolium* like those of coriander. Some species are named after people, such as

P. barklyi, named after the Governor of the Cape of Good Hope, and *P. bowkeri*, which is named after the naturalist who discovered it.

Gardening with species geraniums

Generally species pelargoniums are hardy, grow well, and have less problems from pests and diseases. They have not arisen through hybridization so their propensity for growth has not been compromised by less vigorous genes. The plants are not particularly large or showy, but give sustainable growth and reliable cover.

Groundcover or trailing plants could include *P. alchemilloides* or *P. peltatum* or succulents such as *P. carnosum* and *P. crithmifolium*. Underground tubers are seen in *P. schizopetalum* and *P. appendiculatum*. Shrubby species pelargoniums include the regular *P. zonale* cultivars and those of *P. cucullatum*.

Some species do not look like typical pelargoniums. *P. betulinum* has expanding stems with birch-like leaves. Other species are fascinating by themselves, such as *P. fulgidum* with its long flower stalks and red flowers. The flowers of *P. triste* provide an exquisite scent at dusk. Each could be grown as a pot plant or in a small border.

P. 'kewensis'
LEFT *This is a 'species hybrid', known as 'kewensis', that has a large umbel of bright red flowers. This is borne above the light green-zoned leaves that make up a compact plant. The genetic origin of the term 'species hybrids' is not clear, but the epithet means that it is not a true species.*

P fulgidum
LEFT *This is the other form that has completely different petal colours and the form of the flowers is different too.*

P. inquinans
BELOW *An important species, this is one of the parents of modern zonal pelargoniums (P. x hortorum), the other species being P. zonale. This is quite a vigorous plant*

IVIES

The attractive leaf shapes of ivy-leaved pelargoniums make them popular throughout the garden, with the tiny leaves of miniature varieties being much in demand for pots and hanging baskets.

IVY-LEAVED PELARGONIUMS are subdivided according to flowers, leaves or hybridization: single- and double-flowered, rosettes, fancy-leaved and hybrid ivy-leaved pelargoniums that have originated from crosses between *P. peltatum* and *P. hotorum* such as 'Millfield Gem' (previously known as 'Alliance' and 'Victory'). Examples of the other groups are L'Elégante AGM (single), 'Snowdrift' (double), 'Beauty of Eastbourne' (rosette) and 'Duke of Edinburgh' (fancy-leaved). Old fashioned L'Elégante AGM has much to offer in a hanging basket.

Many trailing pelargoniums have originated from varieties of *P. peltatum* which grows wild in Cape Province, South Africa. One of *P. peltatum's* varieties is *clypeatum* (meaning very pubescent, or downy) and this has been used in the hybridization of many of today's trailing pelargoniums.

Pelargoniums were used by the garden designer Gertrude Jekyll as a contribution to her colour scheme and drifts of colour in herbaceous borders. One new variety at the time, called 'Mme Crousse', was used in borders next to paths; it is now an AGM plant. Working with pelargoniums clarified Jekyll's taste – that bright cultivars had their place in the garden. Jekyll's recommendation for sunny spots in the garden was to use two-year-old pelargoniums in pots to add to the colour. Jekyll's

P. 'Harlequin Mahogany'
ABOVE *The Harlequin series of ivy-leaved pelargoniums produces some interesting cultivars that juxtapose reds with pinks and white. The flowers on the trusses are close together, providing generous blossoms that look wonderful trailing from hanging baskets.*

P. 'Millfield Gem'
RIGHT *This dwarf ivy-leaved pelargonium produces lots of pink flowers with a touch of crimson at the base of the petals.*

P. 'L'Elégante'
ABOVE LEFT
When plants are left without watering the edges of the leaf become more rosy.

P. 'Harlequin Miss Liverbird'
ABOVE *Smaller trusses of flowers in a lighter pink with a larger expanse of white on the petals are typical of this cultivar.*

P. 'Harlequin Ted Day'
ABOVE *Growing as large trusses with an abundance of deep pink smudged with a small amount of white, this grows well in hanging baskets.*

use of ivy-leaved and zonal pelargoniums in a border was innovative. At the time 'Paul Crampel' was used at the back of the border because of its tall growth (its other name was 'Meteor'). Today, new cultivars, such as PACs and PELFIs, produce side shoots early and produce bushier, shorter plants.

Trailing pelargoniums climb if given help. The spectacular double flowers of 'Rouletta' look fine against a wall while 'Harlequin Mahogany' provides a richer flower. Many pelargoniums are complemented by *Helichrysum petiolare*. 'Rio de Balcons Red', 'Carl Red Balcony' and Swiss Balcony' create beautiful floral waterfalls.

'Cascade de Feu' and 'Decora Imperial' brighten up any window box or cascade down a wall. Continental-type ivy-leaved pelargoniums are a mainstay of Mediterranean gardening.

There are many modern, dwarf ivy-leaved pelargoniums ideally suited for hanging baskets, such as 'Santa Paula', 'Snow Queen' and 'Tomboy'. Some of the brightest reds are 'Red Blizzard' and 'Leuche-Cascade', or for delicate pinks 'Sophie Cascade' or 'Rose Mini-Cascade'. More recently a range of ivy-leaved pelargoniums from the east of Germany, called the PAC series, adds an interesting divergence of leaf colour with 'PAC Evka'. This has a cream edge to its leaves and the compact plant has cascading trusses of bright red flowers.

Forgetting to water or feed can have beneficial results. The stress caused by water starvation changes the pigments in the leaf so that attractive pinks appear in place of greens especially around the edges of the leaves. The phenomenon can be seen in varieties such as *P.* L'Elégante AGM.

P. 'PELFI Bright Cascade'

LEFT *Rich dark red typifies this cultivar that is covered in flowers and does well in window boxes.*

P. PELFI 'Lilac Cascade'
LEFT *An ivy-leaved pelargonium that has been awarded its AGM for its reasonable tolerance down to 2°C (33°F).*

P. 'Sofie Cascade'
ABOVE *The narrow petals have thin dark veins toward the base, and the tip of each pale pink petal is notched.*

P. 'Roi de Balcons Red'
LEFT *This ivy-leaved pelargonium is sometimes known as P. 'Hederinum', and joins others in the series that may be lilac or rose.*

P. 'Red Blizzard'
RIGHT *Rich red petals make this one of the brightest reds to have in a hanging basket or window box.*

SCENTED VARIETIES

One of the greatest pleasures in growing pelargoniums is to make a collection of scented ones, as each has a wonderfully distinctive smell.

IT IS ALMOST soporific recalling the different scents that pelargoniums can muster: roses, apricots, pines, citrus, lavender, nutmeg, chocolate, eau de Cologne, apple, mint and strawberry! One – named 'Jello' – accurately mimics the smell of the fruity jelly dessert!

One of the greatest pleasures in growing pelargoniums is to make a collection of scented ones, as each has a wonderfully distinctive smell. There are around 100 scented pelargoniums, of which at least a dozen are true species that have naturally occurring scents. Many of the truest scents belong to species pelargoniums, such as the apple pelargoniums (*P. odorissimum*) or the rose-scented *P. graveolens*, which is the source of many commercial oils. Fragrant pelargoniums can be divided into five basic scents: rose, mint, lemon and citrus, fruit and nut and pungent-scented. Apart from the species pelargoniums, the remaining scented pelargoniums can be very loosely divided into groups, those with entire or lobed leaves and those with leaves variously divided and sub-divided. Examples of the first group include *P. variegatum* 'Crispum', *P.* 'Lady Mary' and *P.* 'Brunswick'. The second group includes *P.* 'Joy Lucille' and *P. denticulatum* 'Filicifolium'. Both *P.* 'Attar of Roses' and *P.* 'Lady Plymouth' AGM have highly lobed leaves. There are some very attractive variegated varieties, including *P.* 'Lady Plymouth' AGM, *P. crispum* 'Variegatum', *P. fragrans* group and *P.* 'Creamy Nutmeg'.

Ideally, position these plants where you can enjoy their unrivalled perfumes – brushing past them along a path to release the scent from the leaves or on a small deck or table near a back door where you can pinch the odd leaf as you pass.

SCENTED PELARGONIUMS

This is a selected list of some of the best scented pelargoniums with a description of their scents. Scents are notoriously difficult to describe, but are at least tenacious in pelargoniums. Not all scented pelargoniums have common names, but the names are given where appropriate.

Species (Latin name)	Common name	Scented parts	Description of scent
P. 'Ardwick Cinnamon'		leaves	cinnamon
P. 'Atomic Snowflake'		leaves	Cologne mint
P. 'Attar of Roses'		leaves	lemon
P. 'Camphor Rose'		leaves	camphor
P. capitatum	Rose-scented pelargonium	leaves	rose
P. 'Chantilly'		leaves	orange
P. 'Chocolate Peppermint' A.G.M. (syn. 'Chocolate Tomentosum'	Peppermint pelargonium	leaves	chocolate peppermint
P. 'Concolor Lace'		leaves	light hazel
P. 'Creamy Nutmeg'	Creamy nutmeg pelargonium	leaves	creamy nutmeg, pine
P. Crispum Major		leaves	lemon
P. 'Deerwood Lavender Lad'		leaves	lavender
P. fragrans		leaves	pine
P. graveolens	Sweet scented pelargonium	leaves	orange scent, lemon
P. grossularoides	Coconut pelargonium	leaves	lemony
P. 'Jello'		leaves	American 'jellO'
P. 'Joy Lucille'		leaves	spicy rose
P. odoratissimum	Apple pelargonium	leaves	apple mint
P. 'Rober's Lemon Rose'		leaves	Turkish Delight
P. 'Triste'		flowers	musk

P. 'Creamy Nutmeg'
ABOVE *The two-tone leaves of cream with nutmeg sum up the appeal of this cultivar, which has small white flowers. It is also known as 'Variegated Fragrans'.*

P. 'Joy Lucille'
LEFT *This larger form of scented pelargonium has leaves divided into at least five lobes.*

P. denticulatum 'Filicifolium'
RIGHT *Named after its very narrowly divided leaves, this plant has small pale purple flowers.*

P. 'Crispum Variegatum' AGM
ABOVE *Also called 'French Lace' and 'Variegated Prince Rupert', this has scented leaves with very pronounced variations and makes a good subject in a summer border.*

P. 'Attar of Roses'
RIGHT *Introduced into the UK in about 1900, this cultivar has light green leaves that when touched release a not unfamiliar rose scent. The light pink-purple flowers are small and borne in small groups.*

While all have scented leaves, one variety has scented flowers: the night-scented *P. triste* is a beautiful plant, despite its sad name. The leaves of scented pelargoniums, however, are their chief claim to fame, and there is a wealth of foliage to choose from: tiny curled leaves, finely divided fronds, oak-leaf shapes or spiky. *P.* 'Chocolate Peppermint' has chocolate colours on its large leaves and gives off the mint scent its name suggests.

The great variety of scents is an expression of the natural biodiversity of plants that defend themselves from leaf-eaters in the wild, so you will not be surprised to find that scented pelargoniums do not suffer from leaf-eating pests! Many insect pests are repelled by scented pelargoniums.

There are many ways to use scented pelargoniums. One or two specimens can be planted around entrances and corners, or grown as a collection to create a formidable array of foliage in myriad shapes and colours. Scented varieties are versatile when used in containers, as they can be moved around the garden to perfume different areas. Some of the larger varieties, such as *P.* 'Chocolate Peppermint' AGM or *P.* 'Royal Oak' AGM, can reach up to 1m (40in) across. These can be dug into borders for the summer months and allowed to interweave with other plants, then overwintered indoors in very cold climates.

P. 'Robers Lemon Rose'

ABOVE *The flowers are quite large compared to many scented-leaved cultivars, and are pale pink. The scent is of strong lemon and the plant grows to a medium size. Ideal as a pot plant on a patio or deck.*

P. 'Chocolate Peppermint' AGM

LEFT *Also called 'Bronze Tomentosa', or more often 'Chocolate Tomentosum', this cultivar has a scent of peppermint, not chocolate. It is growing here with pink-flowered 'PAC Rose Evka'.*

P. 'Prince of Orange'
LEFT *This cultivar looks more like an ivy-leaved pelargonium.*

P. 'Madame Auguste Nonin'
ABOVE *The flowers are grouped together like those of a miniature regal, and the petals are a combination of red and white*

P. 'Brunswick' AGM
LEFT *Bold red flowers with a distinct dark smudging in the centre of the petals typify this cultivar.*

P. 'Attar of Roses'
RIGHT *This obliging cultivar grows well outside during a temperate winter or in a greenhouse or conservatory. It can become very leggy and will quickly build up to become a substantial plant.*

ZONALS

ZONAL PELARGONIUMS typify the garden pelargonium as most know it. They can be used indoors, in window boxes, hanging baskets or in borders. This versatility combined with their speedy growth in optimum conditions has contributed to their success. *P.* 'Deacon Birthday', 'PELFI Noblesse' and the dwarf 'Rev Stringer' are all good garden performers. Zonal pelargoniums, as we know them today, make up a collection of bright and beautiful plants, the major group of garden pelargoniums. There are many different types but they all have various characteristics that bring them together as zonals. Typically they are upstanding, erect plants with stiff succulent stems, and fairly rounded leaves. Flowers can be single, double or semi-double.

P. 'Green Ears'
ABOVE *This stellar zonal has deeply cut foliage and flowers that perform well in the garden and flower continuously.*

P. 'Vina'
RIGHT *Growing as a dwarf, this cultivar has double flowers in apricot with bronze foliage.*

LEAF MARKINGS

The zone is a particularly striking feature of the leaf and is highly variable. It generally takes a uniform position around the heart-shaped leaf and is set well inside the leaf margin. Some varieties have thin zones, while others have thicker, progressing as far as the centre.

THE ZONE, whether light or dark, narrow or thick, effectively highlights and contrasts the marginal part of the leaf, which may be green, white or cream. The darker the zone, the brighter the marginal area appears, perhaps endorsing the theory that this form of marking provides camouflage for the plant by helping to break up the outline of the leaf, and thus deterring grazers. Whatever their purpose, gardeners are always keen to acquire these distinctive and very attractive zonals for garden display.

Some of the best-known zonals include 'Frank Headley' AGM, 'Dolly Varden' AGM and 'Mrs Henry Cox' AGM. It is no coincidence that many choice zonals have been awarded the prestigious Award of Garden Merit (AGM), bestowed upon outstanding plants by the Royal Horticultural Society of London. 'Betwixt' is an unusual cultivar to have in the garden, since it has leaves that are upturned at the edges, which can make it look diseased. However, it is a vigorous plant with a mass of red flowers.

The zones of the pelargonium leaf can be very pale, as in 'Susie Q' or 'Crystal Palace Gem' AGM, or they can be very dark as in 'Mrs Farren', 'Bronze Corrine' (bronze) or 'Marechal MacMahon'. Sometimes the dark zones are tinged with red as in 'Dolly Varden' AGM or 'Contrast'. A central green zone with light cream margins can be seen in 'Mrs J.C. Mapping' AGM, 'Hills of Snow', 'Ivory Snow', 'Madame Salleron' AGM, 'Madame Butterfly' and 'Mont Blanc'. The names of these cultivars provide many references to the whiteness of the leaf margins.

P. 'Mont Blanc'
ABOVE *This delightful cultivar has single white flowers and a dwarf growth habit.*

P. 'Dolly Varden' AGM
LEFT *The pink and red forms of this cultivar have single flowers that are excellent for use in containers.*

P. 'Susie Q'
LEFT *These apple green leaves are large and regular in shape, but with an irregular and somewhat diffused purple chestnut zone. The single flowers are equally large and salmon pink. It makes a very attractive plant, growing to about 30cm (12in) high and 30cm (12in) across, and is ideal in a window box or as a patio plant.*

P. 'Mrs. Farren'
RIGHT *Fifty years ago there were over 50 pelargoniums that had the epithet 'Mrs'; now at least 50 percent of these plants have been lost.*

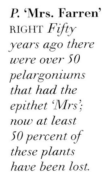

P. 'Mrs. J. C. Mappin' AGM
LEFT *The silver variegated foliage is complemented by white flowers that have a pink eye.*

P. 'Madame Butterfly'
ABOVE *The purity of the colours in this variegated cultivar are impressive, with the silver variegated leaves contrasting with the dark crimson double flowers.*

FANCY LEAVES

*The term 'fancy-leaved' encompasses the natural and contrived
variation in leaf shape and colour of pelargoniums that includes the
visually-stimulating golden-leaved varieties.*

THERE IS A natural propensity for living things to produce colour variations, thanks to the random mixing of genetic material through pollination. In addition, variations are produced by plantsmen seeking to come up with the unusual.

The Victorians endeavoured to create more strictly golden-margined pelargoniums. One of the earliest grown in the UK from about 1820 was 'Golden Chain', thought to be a sport from *P. inquinans*. After the mid-nineteenth century two other important golden-leaved pelargoniums were produced, 'Mrs Pollock' and 'Lady Cullum', both generated from 'Golden Tom Thumb'. This started a craze for golden and bronze cultivars.

The term 'golden tricolour' is sometimes used to describe golden plants that have three colours on the same plant, i.e. golden and green leaves and coloured flowers. 'Golden Brilliantissimum' has been a long-standing favourite. Yellow and bronze is very striking by itself and is even more pronounced with, for example, scarlet flowers. 'Freak of Nature' is a bizarre plant that supports stems entirely given over to off-white patches on its leaves, as if liberally splashed with paint, while other leaves are green. 'Bristol' and 'Mrs Strang' have green leaves with yellow margins. 'Mr Henry Cox' AGM is a stalwart with red bronze zones, closely followed by 'Bronze Corrine' and 'Contrast'.

There have been many contributions of golden-leaved stellar cultivars in North America. In Canada in 1986, Ian Gillam – who later bred 'Golden Ears' and 'Mrs Pat' – developed 'Vancouver Centennial' to celebrate Expo. Others were developed in the USA including 'Green Gold Kleine Liebling', 'Peppermint Star' and 'Rusty'. England also produced many stunning goldens, such as Ray Bidwell's 'Chattisham' or 'Elmsett' or 'Holbrook', named after villages in Suffolk.

P. 'Mrs Strang'
ABOVE *Known from at least the 1880s, this is an old and established cultivar that is classified as a golden tricolour because of its leaf colours. 'Mrs Strang' carries double orange flowers that contrast well with its light honey-coloured leaves.*

P. 'Mr Henry Cox' AGM
RIGHT *The painter's pallete seems to have been mixed together to create this gay assemblage of colour. The flowers are small with pale pink petals that are often notched.*

ZONAL FLOWERS

Zonals are not just worth growing for their striking foliage, they also produce some wonderful flowers in a variety of colours. A warming climate is allowing temperate gardeners to dabble in more Mediterranean plantings in the garden.

Orange-coloured pelargoniums, most of which are zonals, make a striking addition to the garden and are very popular. They range in colour from delicate, pale salmon flowers such as 'Orange Splash' to vibrant, hot oranges that are almost red, like the flowers of 'Majola'. The orange range brings together some single-flowered cultivars such as 'Gazelle' and semi-doubles such as 'Diana Palmer' or 'Elizabeth Angus', with its large floppy flowers.

There are at least three unusual orange pelargoniums: 'Els' with aquilegia-like leaves (formossum hybrids with 'finger' type leaves) and stellar flowers; 'Majola' with convoluted petals which make up a rose- or camelia-like flower; and 'Orange Splash', which is one of the new generation of pelargoniums. It has broken patterns on its petals which burst out with irregular splashes, streaks and spots. 'Splashed' flowers are very collectible, and you could combine different colours. Other orange pelargoniums include 'Deacon Coral Reef', 'Meadowside Orange', 'Orangesonne' and 'PELFI Tango Orange'.

P. 'Gazelle'
ABOVE *Single, pale orange flowers are borne on large rounded trusses from the dark green, zonal foliage of this fancy-leaved pelargonium.*

P. 'Els'
LEFT *The petals are thin, and some of the stamens are petaloid (look like petals). The leaves are divided with dark centres.*

P. 'Elizabeth Angus'
LEFT *A zonal pelargonium with large orange flowers on large trusses. The foliage is mid-green.*

P. 'Maloja'
RIGHT *The orange flowers have petals that are unique since they are large and wavy. This cultivar originated in Switzerland.*

P. 'Orange Splash'
RIGHT *One of several cultivars whose petals are broken with different colours. There are a dozen cultivars with the 'Orange' prefix.*

HOT REDS

THERE ARE SOME wonderful hot-red zonals. 'Stadt Bern' has dark crimson flowers named after the city of Berne in Switzerland, set off with dark foliage. 'Happy Thought' AGM (often mis-labelled as 'A Happy Thought') has large round heads of single flowers, and 'Feuerriese' has loose scarlet heads. 'Paul Crampel' is a mainstay of the cottage window box. There are three others with a more open nature, recalling the petals of camellia. These are 'H. Rigler', 'Crimson Fire' and 'Drummer Boy'. Double zonal reds include 'Alex' and 'Jacqueline'.

A vivid display of reds, yellows, greens and whites is produced by many of those classified as variegated red zonals. 'Mangel's Variegated' is a great exhibitor in full sunshine, but cannot keep this up for long as its bright yellow leaves fade, a common failing among yellow-leaved cultivars. Keep them in shade where the reds remain strident and the leaves help brighten up dark areas. They flower well into frost periods before dying back. 'Madame Butterfly' has clear white and green foliage and dark red trusses of bloom. 'Mrs Farren' has darker leaves but is equally red in bloom. 'Freak of Nature' and 'Happy Thought' AGM can jazz up a border with their outlandish displays.

P. 'Hildegard'
ABOVE *Large trusses of bright red to orange semi-double flowers are borne on stout stems above medium-sized plants.*

P. 'Crimson Fire'
ABOVE *As its name describes, the flowers are brightest red and the trusses of flowers are compact.*

P. 'H. Rigler'
LEFT *This zonal has trusses of close-knit semi-double flowers in hot red.*

P. 'Stadt Bern'
LEFT *One of the brightest of the zonals, this plant grows to medium height and can be usefully employed in baskets and tubs.*

P. 'Paul Crampel'
ABOVE *This still-popular zonal adorned many window boxes in the early nineteenth century.*

P. 'Happy Thought' AGM
LEFT *Known erroneously as 'A Happy Thought' this has brightly coloured zonal foliage that contrasts with its bright red flowers.*

P. 'Penny Serenade'
LEFT *This dwarf pelargonium has fairly open trusses of bright red flowers and green leaves.*

P. 'Bristol'
LEFT *With pronounced zonal markings on its wavy leaves, this cultivar has bright red trusses of flowers.*

HIGHFIELDS

Highfields boast some of the most beautiful varieties of pelargoniums available and occur in a wonderful variety of colours and flower shapes.

HIGHFIELDS PELARGONIUMS ARE noted for their beauty. They were originally bred by Ken Gamble and the semi-double 'Highfields Pink', an Irene seedling, was introduced by Gamble in 1967. There are other pelargoniums introduced by Gamble that do not have the Highfields prefix, including 'Annette Kellerman' and 'Queen Ingrid'.

About 40 cultivars now bear the Highfields name. Characteristics include compact growth, abundant large trusses of flowers, many with strident colours, others with beautiful pastel shades. They can only be propagated from cuttings, but this is not difficult. Many beds, borders and window boxes would be poorer but for Highfields pelargoniums; 'Highfields Flair' is an excellent bedder.

Highfields occur as single-flowered, semi-double and double-flowered cultivars. Typical singles include 'Highfields Appleblosson' in cerise-pink 'Highfields Pride' in red or 'Highfields Supreme' in bright red with a white eye. Typical semi-doubles include 'Highfields Orange' and doubles include 'Highfields Charisma' in salmon-pink, or 'Highfields Attracta' in soft pink.

Their round, compact nature is well-illustrated by 'Highfields Cameo', 'Highfields Flair', 'Highfields Pink' and 'Highfields Snowdrift'. 'Highfields Ballerina' offers an alternative look with its attractive dark foliage.

P. 'Highfields Attracta'
ABOVE *While only faintly aromatic, the flowers of this pelargonium are particularly vibrant and it flowers for a long period.*

P. 'Highfields Orange'
ABOVE *Typical of the Highfields cultivars, the flower trusses are large and of fairly uniform colour.*

P. 'Highfields Snowdrift'
LEFT *Balled together, the flowers of this cultivar are generally white, not an abundant colour across the whole range of pelargoniums.*

P. 'Highfields Appleblossom'
OPPOSITE *These flower trusses bear lots of single flowers close together in pinky cream, as the name suggests.*

ROSEBUDS AND TULIPS

The propensity of some pelargoniums to jam all their flowers together into one tight ball of buds was easily captured by the Victorian pelargonium enthusiasts, and what a delight they are – appleblossom, roses and tulips combined.

IN 1870 THE first Rosebuds, 'Appleblossom Rosebud', Red Rambler' and 'Scarlet Rambler' were released. In rosebuds the buds are crammed in so tightly they cannot open as flowers, and the ball of buds is otherwise called a 'noisette' presumably after the rose hybrid of that name, and originally from the French word for 'hazelnut'.

These zonals combine the subtleties of roses and apple blossom into their looks, but not their scents. The buds in 'Appleblossom' are a suffusion of pale pink, white with a dash of pale green in the centre, mimicking some of the colour stages of apple blossom. Interesting new varieties include *P.* 'PELFI Summer Red Rose' and 'Summer Lila Rose', both of which are ivy-leaved rosebuds.

Strident reds are seen in 'Scarlet Rambler Rosebud Gem Double Rose' – which in fact look like tight buds of roses – and in 'Red Pandora'. In terms of tulip look-alikes, 'Patricia Andrea' carries this off well. Its flowers are tighter than any rosebud, and are so perfect they look almost unreal.

Three ramblers in this group vary in flower colour – the 'Red Rambler' with blood red flowers, 'Spanish Rambler' with muted crimson, and the darker still 'Plum Rambler' (now called 'Rosebud'), which has purple flowers.

P. 'Appleblossom Rosebud'
ABOVE *Bunched like tiny appleblossoms, or a Provence rose, the flowers never open because they are made up of many tiny petals. Having become popular in the late nineteenth century, there are now many cultivars of similar shape.*

P. 'Plum Rambler'
RIGHT *The rich colours of these double blossoms are hard to beat. It takes off like a rampant rose in a warm climate and should survive the winter in a greenhouse.*

P. 'Patricia Andrea'

LEFT *This is a vigorous tulip-flowered pelargonium, with tight buds gathered into an appealing ball of colour.*

Variety of 'Appleblossom Rosebud'
ABOVE *Typical of the rosebud group of zonal pelargoniums this old cultivar makes an exquisite picture of pink and white.*

P. 'Red Pandora'

RIGHT *Deep red flowers of this tulip-flowered pelargonium make this a complete look-alike for a double rose.*

COMMERCIAL SERIES

The proliferation of pelargoniums is a controversial subject, but there is no doubting the beauty of some of the stunning commercially-bred pelargoniums.

THE OBSCURE ORIGIN of many commercially-bred pelargoniums has led some authorities to dismiss terms such as 'Fiats', 'Irenes', 'Ricards' or 'Bruant Types' as meaningless. Many breeders have not catalogued crosses or disagree with each other. 'Bruant Types' and 'Ricards' have now sadly disappeared, but 'Fiat' and 'Irene' series are still available, and have been joined by the 'Video' series.

PACs and PELFIs are named after nurseries in Germany, and use the nursery name as a prefix, as in 'PAC Rosepen'. These are widely available in most garden centres in the UK and Europe.

Irenes and Fiats are available from specialist nurseries. American 'Irenes' may have had a French 'Fiat' as a parent and are robust, fast growing and free-flowering with semi-double or double flowers. The 'Video' series have rather pedestrian names such as 'Video Rose', 'Video Scarlet' and 'Video Salmon'.

The 'Unique' series (rudely pluralized to 'Uniques') are stout and shrubby, and some produce scent. The flowers are often reddish and borne on umbels. 'Madame Nonin' and 'Paton's Unique' are red, but flowers can be pink, mauve or white, as in 'White Unique' or purple 'Rollison's Unique'.

P. 'Toyon'
ABOVE *This zonal has uniformly shaped petals that make for very simple and uncluttered flowers.*

P. 'Irene'
ABOVE *Awarded its AGM for being a worthy herbaceous perennial that can tolerate minimum temperatures down to 2° C (33°F), this has orange-coloured flowers borne on fairly loose trusses.*

P. 'Rosepen'
LEFT *A zonal double, this has magenta flowers borne on loose trusses.*

P. 'Video Salmon'

RIGHT *There are a number of plain colours in the Video series to meet every designer's eye. This one has an overall salmon colour mixed with areas of lightness.*

P. 'Video Rose'

ABOVE *With white eyes, the rose-coloured petals are a uniform shape that give a soothing symmetrical feel to these simple flowers.*

P. 'Video Scarlet'

RIGHT *Burning in scarlet, the petals of this cultivar uphold the reds typical of so many pelargoniums in all sorts of groups.*

P. 'Fiat Supreme'

ABOVE *The flowers of this double zonal are various shades of apricot.*

P. 'Fiat'

RIGHT *Among the several in this series, this is the straight Fiat with apricot-orange double flowers in an open truss.*

STELLARS, STARTELS AND CACTI

Stellars introduce an antipodean or exotic perspective, since many of the Stellar series were bred by T. Both from Adelaide, Western Australia. These include such niceties as 'Stellar Arctic Star' (now known as 'Arctic Star'), 'Stellar Snowflake' and 'Stellar Orange'.

STELLAR FLOWERS ARE single or double, often with wedge-shaped petals, and often narrow or forked upper petals with serrated or crimped edges. There are also dwarf forms such as 'Fandango' in cerise red, 'Queen Ester' with an array of purple and white shown off by the wing-like green sepals, or the miniature 'Els' in salmon that also has aquilegia-shaped leaves. Stellars are also called finger-flowered pelargoniums since the deeply lobed leaves give the appearance of fingers.

One of the most widespread and most well-known stellars is 'Vancouver Centennial' AGM, known for the dark colour variations of its leaves. The single flowers, borne on fairly open trusses, are salmon-orange with typically two forked petals and two larger toothed ones. Another useful stellar in hanging baskets or in pots is 'Bird Dancer' AGM.

Seed merchants Thompson & Morgan produced the 'Startel' series. It is a zonal stellar cultivar, a fancy-leaved pelargonium and a dwarf.

Cacti pelargoniums (also called Poinsettia-flowering) have more divided petals than stellars. The massed flowers make up a ball, like a spiky cactus with thin petals, such as 'Mrs Salter Bevis' (a dwarf) or 'Mini-Czech' (a miniature) and have normal zonal-type foliage.

P. 'Queen Ester'
ABOVE *Classified as a zonal double stellar, this has some of the more bizarre shapes found in pelargoniums.*

P. 'Arctic Star'
LEFT *The petals of this pure white single stellar would do well in any small garden with a white theme.*

P. 'Pagoda'
RIGHT *Clothed in chintzy pink, the large trusses of this stellar are very attractive.*

P. 'Els'
LEFT *The soft pink petals of the many flowers make an attractive ring of colour in this stellar cultivar.*

P. 'Red Soldier'
ABOVE *The very finely divided petals were probably the inspiration for the name of this cultivar.*

SINGLE DWARFS

While miniatures have been known for over 180 years, dwarfs have only really been around as a recognized group for about 30 years. The availability of less costly greenhouses in the second half of the twentieth century may have contributed to their recent level of popularity.

DWARFS MUST BE no smaller than 12cm (5 in) but not taller than 20cm (8 in), and for showing, not in a pot greater than 11cm (4.5in) in diameter. However, dwarfs are usually sold to grow into 30cm (12in), and miniatures to 15-17cm (6-7in). As soon as a miniature outgrows this size it becomes a dwarf. Exhibition rules may be strict but nature does not fit easily into these criteria. Thus it is clear that the terms easily overlap and in some cases are used for each other.

Many dwarfs have dark leaves, possibly because they originate from dark-leaved zonals. Two dark-leaved pelargoniums may be responsible for the colouring of many miniatures and dwarfs: 'Mme Fournier' and 'Red Black Vesuvius'. The initial enthusiam for small varieties in the early 1900s was renewed in the late 1940s with miniature fancy-leaved varieties. 'Silver Kewense' was introduced in 1956 with silver and green leaves.

Stellars, as zonals, both single- and double-flowered, also have dwarf characteristics, although this is exceeded in some cultivars. 'Apricot', grows to 45cm (18in) which is too tall for exhibition. 'Peppermint Star' has small globes of small flowers attractively colored in white and cerise. 'Pink Gold Ears' has pale pink single flowers. One of the most popular varieties is 'Bird Dancer' AGM. 'Vancouver Centennial' AGM is classified as a dwarf, but in warmer climates it can grow to 1m (40in) in a hanging basket.

Other series of dwarfs and miniatures include Occold Varieties, Rivers Range, Deacon Varieties, Brookside Varieties and Miniature Ivy-leaved. Nearly all are classified as miniatures. If ultimate miniaturization is being sought, these cultivars should be avoided. Another significant group of dwarfs and miniatures is the 'Suffolk Villages' series, with over 60 varieties.

P. 'Occold Tangerine'
ABOVE *This unusually coloured pelargonium would make a real splash in the garden. The Occold series are noted for their flower colors.*

P. 'Vancouver Centennial' AGM
RIGHT *This dwarf stellar has single red flowers and unique foliage. The size of the plant will vary according to your local climate.*

P. 'Festal'
ABOVE *The rose-pink flowers of this miniature cultivar, that errs on the semi-double side of being single, are grouped together as a small truss, producing a pleasing effect.*

P. 'Peppermint Star'
ABOVE *The petals of this dwarf stellar are arranged to give the impression of a star shape, hence its name. The pink towards the end of the petals is very attractive in this large zonal stellar.*

P. 'Pink Golden Ears'
LEFT *This pelargonium is named after its soft pink flowers whose petals are significantly notched. It is a dwarf stellar pelargonium.*

DOUBLE DWARFS

With their luscious full flowers and intense shows of colour, it is no wonder that double dwarfs are such a favourite with gardeners. Whether you are growing them as exhibition plants or simply to brighten up a border, they are well worth adding to your collection.

MORE DOUBLE-FLOWERED dwarfs occur than single-flowered, or so it would seem. There is a group of dwarfs called 'Norfolk Dwarfs' which demonstrates the reverse, where in fact only about a third of the 33 varieties have double flowers.

Double-flowered dwarfs make excellent exhibition subjects because they are compact and look gorgeous, almost like miniature roses, such as 'Bold Carmine' and 'Claydon'. 'Little Alice' has tangerine-coloured flowers and an AGM accolade. 'Vina' has apricot-coloured flowers and yellowish foliage.

All the Deacons are dwarfs and have double-flowers. There are 27 varieties that occur in various pastel shades, some with beautiful golden leaves. Being so small they are excellent for bedding out or growing in pots and containers. The double flowers are borne on neat and compact trusses that are raised up above the foliage. There is a pureness and uniformity in colours of the different cultivars, which sets them apart from other series. The pastel shades on offer should fit neatly into any garden planner's palette so these are extremely useful plants to have in the garden. Examples of such purity in colour include the delicate yet striking neon pink of 'Deacon Romance', the salmon pink of 'Deacon Trousseau', the pale orange of 'Deacon Sunburst', or the bright orange of 'Deacon Summertime', 'Deacon Golden Bonanza' has the extra advantage of golden leaves to complement its rose-like petals. Double-flowered stellar dwarfs include 'Pagoda', 'Prim' and 'Super Nova'.

P. 'Prima Donna'
ABOVE *Tight trusses of double pink-red flowers make this dwarf pelargonium ideal for showing.*

P. 'Deborah Miliken'
RIGHT *The massed heads of this zonal double are attractive, and the particular way in which the petals are twisted and convoluted in each flower is intriguing.*

P. 'Bold Carmine'
LEFT *Some of the reddish blossoms are shown off in this compact double-flowered dwarf that is ideal as an exhibition plant.*

P. 'Eileen'
ABOVE *This is an exhibition-type dwarf which produces a profusion of lovely orange flowers with petals that overlap each other.*

P. 'Little Alice'
AGM
LEFT *Small orange double flowers are produced on a dwarf plant, creating an effect that is worthy of any exhibition or garden. The foliage is very dark bronze.*

REGALS

I IT IS THE FLOWERS that make regals so special. They are large and often produced in vast quantities. Regals make wonderful show plants. Colours vary from white through pink, mauve and purple to red, while shapes can be as simple as a pansy, fringed, small and rounded, or with a wavy petal edge. There has been a great awakening of regals in the last few years, both in North America and in England, and scores of new cultivars have been introduced.

The way that regals have been treated in this book is by colour, which seems to have been established as the usual way of looking at regals. Here the various colour persuasions chosen, almost entirely subjectively, are hot, cool, and finally the dramatic butes.

P. 'Silvia'
ABOVE *These flowers are fairly large with slightly wavy margins to the petals and dark colourings down the throat.*

P. 'Rembrandt'
RIGHT *Dark and mysterious, this regal was raised in 1972 and its petals are full with rich royal purple, cherry and mauve, all in the shape of a giant pansy.*

HOT COLOURS

Hot colours will always have an appeal for the gardener. Their sheer impact in a border or container makes them impossible to ignore. The Regals provide plenty of options when looking for hot-coloured pelargoniums.

REDS ARE WELL-EXPRESSED by pelargoniums. There are many shades of red in regals sitting between the salmons and the darkest of all regals. Red regals are often suffused with tinges of dark colour and very many of them cannot throw off the dark throat markings and go 100 percent red.

Those that try the hardest to provide a pure red colour include 'Grand Slam' (introduced in 1950), 'Jewell' and 'Lamorna'. 'Linda' and 'Silvia' have distinctly rounded red petals and the flowers are agreeably close together to make a fine display. Ruffled petals are seen especially in 'Souvenir' and 'Fiery Sunrise', both of which have a touch of orange about their reds, and 'Souvenir' is suffused with lightness in its throat.

As we move from the reds to the darker-coloured regals, it is interesting to note the dark throat of 'Red Susan Pearl' and how this develops into the dark uppers of 'Spot on Bonanza', 'Belvedere' and 'Rimfire' — the latter introduced in 1999.

Salmon is a common and popular colour among the regals, providing a change from red, while maintaining the hot impact. The strongest salmon is seen in 'Lustre' with its masses of flowers that are well-ruffled, each set hard against each other. Simple pansy-like flowers with a clear salmon hue are seen in 'Gottenburg' which also has a dark throat on the uppers. 'Pink Bonanza' is a delicate pinky-orange with off-white blushing and a darker area on the base of the upper petals.

The popular 'Aztec' AGM has a dark throat to its pinkish petals. Fringing of the petals is seen in at least one variety. 'Aztec' makes a good show plant since it is a compact plant. The darkness on the uppers is carried to extremes in 'Royal Star', which has an attractive lighter frill around the upper petals with the rest pale salmon pink. 'Neon Maid' is more open, large and lighter with its pansy-like flowers of rich salmon surrounding a white throat. There are so many from which to choose — 'Gefora Peach' and 'Fiery Salmon' have their own charm.

P. 'Hazel Choice'

LEFT *There are over 30 different hazels in this series, of very many colours with large flowers and compact growth. The original hazel was 'Hazel' with deep purple colours.*

G. 'Voo Doo'
LEFT *The dark red colours of the small, slightly reflexed petals surround the dark centre. Many of the regals have dark centres and these may be filled with contrasting colour, blotched, veined or spotted. It also appears in some catalogues as a hybrid of 'Unique'.*

P. 'Aztec'
ABOVE *Raised in 1947, this is a semi-double zonal pelargonium with orange-red petals. A popular cultivar on account of its strong constitution, it has bunches of wavy flowers that make a big impression.*

P. 'Neon Maid'
ABOVE *The neon-pink flowers with their white eyes and frilly petals make this an ideal competition plant, or focus specimen for the garden.*

COOL COLOURS

White, pink and purple zonals bring a calming, gentle injection of colour to the garden.
Although many of the flowers are not pure in colour, they provide the
desired overall cool effect.

SUCH IS THE VARIETY of colour within the regals that a selection is simply arbitrary and hugely subjective. This can only scratch the surface and provide a vignette into this huge world of manmade biodiversity. Pelargonium genes are capable of just as many interesting and colourful combinations in the future as have gone before. Pure white pelargoniums are hard to find. The petals of 'Turtles White' may be blotched, and 'Volante National Alba' has lavender tints. A popular variety in the U.S. is 'White Champion', which has large white flowers with pink blushing. 'Jasmine' has pure petal colour but red-wine-coloured marks down its throat. It can also have tiny marks on its petals. 'Super Spot Bonanza' can swap white petals for all pink petals just to upset the continuous swathes of white.

A suffusion of pink is typical in many of the white-flowered regals. It is obvious in 'Cherie', which has a purple smudge on its upper petals, or in 'Joan Morf', which has a defined pink suffusion in the middle of its lower petals. Pink develops well in these light-coloured regals with 'Mona Lisa' and 'Pearly Primrose', both of which have purple blotches on the uppers. Among the Hazels, 'Hazel Frills' has ruffled petals and a pronounced red veining that is the mirror image of its stamens and anthers.

Pinks and purples are notoriously difficult to describe throughout the botanical world, and pelargoniums are no exception. It is perhaps no accident that two of the AGM regals fall into this loose basket of colour. *P.* 'Carisbrooke' AGM is a pink and carmine-flowered regal that used to

P. 'Spot on Bonanza'
LEFT *The flowers are large and frilly with irregular pink markings on the upper petals and purple spots on the lower petals.*

P. 'Hazel Frills'
BELOW *Overall the truss of flowers is very compact, being mostly white with red markings down the throat.*

be called 'Ballerina'. It was given its Award of Merit (AGM) in 1952 for its 'phlox pink' and 'rose pink' ruffled flowers. It had arisen earlier as a seedling of 'Queen Mary' in 1928 – this latter cultivar is no longer available.

P. 'Lavender Grand Slam' AGM – its colour speaking for itself – has the most uniform of colours across its large ruffled petals. It was originally selected in 1953 as a sport that had arisen from 'Grand Slam', which itself was raised in 1950 with purple and mauve colours. 'Salmon Slam' carries the general pattern and flower structure of the other slams, but with a strong suffusion of salmon-orange colour across its petals. A mere twitch of the gene sequence produces this dramatic colour difference. Named

after the effect of seeing such magnificent pelargoniums in flower, the Grand Slams have a big reputation that precedes them.

Other pure-pink regals include 'Fruhlingser Lilac', 'Lilac Jewell', 'Prince' and 'Susan Pearce'. A regal purple that has smaller flowers and the appearance of being very ruffled is 'Claydon Firebird', while 'Rosemaroy' (not to be be confused with zonal 'Rosemary' and zonal dwarf 'Rosemarie') is more open with its ruffleness but still has a dark purple throat. 'Peter's Choice' is a remarkable cultivar with large flowers and a whitish throat. 'Rembrandt' has a magnificent deep purple almost velvet, appearance over most of its petals with only a light purple margin to break it up.

P. 'Carisbrooke' AGM
LEFT *This used to be called 'Ballerina', probably because its frilly pink petals recall a ballerina's tutu. The dark throat is distinctive amid the large pink petals. It grows to become a very large plant.*

P. 'Claydon Firebird'
RIGHT *In this cultivar the flowers are packed together and the petals are very wavy. The basic colour of the petals is purple going to a deep purple toward the throat.*

BUTES

*The dark sombre colours of regals are rather appealing and have certainly
proved a hit with gardeners.*

THE EARLIEST BUTE is 'Lord Bute' which attained AGM status in 1910. Formally called 'Purple Robe', it is dressed in velvety purple black with a thin purple-red rim. Rarely seen today is 'Black Magic', which has totally black petals. 'Thundercloud' is also black. Other black regals usually have a tinge of another colour; 'Brown's Butterfly', formerly called 'Black Butterfly' is maroon-black, 'Black Knight' is purple-black, 'Black Velvet' is also purple-black and 'Black Top' is red and black. 'Morwenna' opens as black and takes on a mahogany colour with age.

Other regals with the bute connection are the 'Marchioness of Bute', 'Australian Bute', and 'Dollar Bute'. 'Tashmal' resembles 'Australian Bute' but the trusses grow in a more rosette fashion, and 'Springfield Black' is black velvet set off by a stunning red throat. 'Turkish Coffee' comes nowhere near the darkness of real coffee, but is still an exciting addition to the group.

Other dark regals include 'Romeo', and 'Norgal Regal' with its light centre, maroon petals and ruffled margins dressed in raspberry. Both 'Peggy Sue' and 'South American Bronze' have white-edged petals. 'Marie Rober' takes ruffledness to the extreme with its dark throat and purple petals, while 'Burgundy' is more sombre. 'African Queen' (only available in North America) is superb in containers. Also ideal for containers is 'The Prince' – a miniature with a long blooming period.

P. 'Bushfire'
LEFT *The colour of this regal pelargonium is dark mahogany decorated around the edge or rim of the petals with a contrasting lighter suffusion of dark salmon.*

P. 'Lord Bute' AGM
ABOVE *A classic regal pelargonium and one of many butes, it continues to be widely grown. Once called 'Purple Robe', the petals are purple-black with distinctive fuchsia purple or carmine edges. It is ideal as a bedding plant.*

P. 'Springfield Black'
LEFT *Darker than most, this is one of a dozen cultivars of Springfield regals. The petal shape is irregular, causing the bunching up of each flower.*

ANGELS

Angels started life in the 1820's with a variety called 'Angeline'. They are among the prettiest and most floriferous of the smaller pelargoniums and today the enthusiasm for angels is so great that there are specialist angel growers. If ever there was a group of plants to have fun with, or to collect, it is the angels.

IT IS GENERALLY regarded that two species pelargoniums lent characteristics to angels: *P. crispum* and *P. groussularoides*. Angels are more like regals than zonals. They are miniatures, but not exactly conforming to what we call miniature regals. Angels are bushy and floriferous, reaching no more than 25cm (10in). Individual specimens suit hanging baskets, tubs or window boxes since these delicate plants are not destined for the border. Angels flower through the summer. Most do not have a scent, but a few have retained some; including, 'Imperial Butterfly', 'Mrs G.H. Smith', 'Letitia' and 'Solferino'.

As yet there are no pure-red angels, but 'Velvet Duet' with deep purple and 'Kettle Baston' with its red-purple petals come close, as does 'Jer Rey'. Purples are usually concentrated in the upper petals, as in 'Wayward Angel' AGM or 'Catford Belle' AGM, or smudged in the middle of the flower as in 'Verona Contreras' and 'Sancho Panza'

AGM. 'Captain Starlight' is stunning, especially when mixed in a hanging basket. Some angels are named after English villages and rivers, such as 'Newham Market', 'The Mole', 'The Axe', 'The Tone' and 'The Lyn'.

ANGELS × REGALS (ORIENTALS)

Crosses between angels and regals have resulted in very compact plants with a multitude of flowers including 'Cathay', 'Chintz', 'Kyoto' and 'Rising Sun'. They have been bred for continuous flowering from February to November in temperate climes.

SMALL FLOWERED REGALS

The petals of decorative angels are decorated with spots. The most striking is 'Beronmünster', which has five red spots on its flowers. 'Lara Maid' AGM, 'Sancho Panza' AGM and 'Variegated Mme Layal' AGM are also decorative angels, with the prestigious award of garden merit.

P. 'Gabriel'
LEFT *The relatively small flowers of this plant have carmine uppers and carmine-smudged lowers with a little light-coloured feathering. The overall effect is of dark flowers that would look very appealing in a window box.*

P. 'The Axe'
LEFT *Purple and white make a wonderful contrasting combination. A multitude of these flowers is bound to attract attention.*

P. 'Imperial Butterfly'
ABOVE *Large white petals suggest a butterfly on the wing.*

P. 'Cransley Star'
LEFT *With its two large cerise-red upper petals and the pale pink lower petals, this flower looks like a ruffled pansy.*

P. 'Wayward Angel' AGM
ABOVE *Typical of many angels, this pansy-like cultivar has open flowers with purple smudging on its uppers. It has a lax habit making it ideal for hanging baskets.*

P. 'Sancho Panza' AGM
LEFT *This decorative angel is very striking with a colour scheme that shows off its distant connection to regals; its white rims are very effective.*

DEACONS

A peculiarly English devotion has seen the selection of a group called the deacons that are compact plants ideal for window boxes and hanging baskets.

DEACONS ARE ALL dwarf pelargoniums which were first raised in East Anglia, England by the Reverend Stringer towards the end of the twentieth century. These stunning pelargoniums originated from crosses between miniatures and ivy-leaved pelargoniums. There are almost 30 varieties of deacons available, and they mostly have attractive double flowers. However, there are also a few varieties with semi-double flowers, such as the lovely 'Deacon Summertime'. The nature of one of their parents is clearly evident in their compact habit (which comes from the miniatures) and from their ivy-leaved parents there is a hint of familiarity in the flowers and a waviness of the leaves that is so typical of ivies. However, the doubleness and dwarfness of deacons set them apart from any other group of pelargoniums.

A great variety of traditional colour is represented by the deacons. Colours range from delicate lilac to red, dazzling orange and attractive salmon pink (e.g. 'Deacon Lilac Mist', 'Deacon Regalia', 'Deacon Sunburst' and 'Deacon Trousseau' respectively). 'Deacon Picotee' has a fine purple edging to its white petals. There are also some more unusual colours available for the gardener to try, such as 'Romance', which is a startling neon pink, or 'Deacon Coral Reef' (salmon pink) or 'Deacon Jubilant' (cerise pink). One variety with variegated green and yellow butterfly-mark leaves is 'Deacon Peacock', which also boasts orange-red flowers. Other interesting combinations of colour include 'Deacon Golden Bonanza' with yellow-golden edges to its rounded leaves, and 'Deacon Birthday' with salmon flowers overlaid with peach.

P. 'Deacon Bonanza'
ABOVE *Amongst the more unusual colours, this cultivar has tight clusters of rose flowers whose petals are somewhat ruffled and tightly drawn together.*

P. 'Deacon Coral Reef'
LEFT *The flowers of this deacon are coral pink to apricot, making a superb flowering display.*

Other varieties that you might consider using to create a stunning display on the patio include 'Deacon Arlon', which has elegant white flowers; 'Deacon Flamingo' with stunning orange-scarlet flowers; 'Deacon Moonlight' with pale lilac pink flowers; 'Suntan', which is dressed in pale orange; 'Deacon Summertime' with scarlet red flowers and 'Deacon Romance' with its stunning neon-pink blooms.

One of the virtues of gardening with deacons is that they are dwarf in habit and they do not outgrow the container you plant them in. Being decidedly pretty in their dwarf compaction, with the added attraction of offering a great range of bright and colourful flowers all concentrated together, they make excellent subjects in pots, both for showing at exhibitions or simply to give pleasure around the home and garden. Easy to grow in window boxes where they can be admired from within the house, they can also be grown in hanging baskets and around the edges of large pots and containers. As they are small plants, it is a good idea to display deacons in baskets at eye-level. This means that they can easily be admired for their beauty and it provides an alternative way of showing off exciting plants in the garden. Deacons can also be bedded out in the summer if you wish, but only attempt this if you have enough space for them to excel in their own right. It would be a terrible shame if these beautiful little pelargoniums were to be swamped by exuberant adjacent plantings such as alchemillas, salvias or asters. Wherever you choose to plant them, Deacons will reward you with a display of colour that is almost unrivalled in the world of pelargoniums.

P. 'Deacon Constancy'
LEFT *Clusters of soft pink flowers, either all white or with white, mark out this cultivar. The pastel shades are typical of the group.*

P. 'Deacon Clarion
ABOVE *Deep pink flowers with the petals bunched close together make this double-flowered dwarf quite a spectacle.*

P. 'Deacon Lilac Mist'
LEFT *Loose double flowers with pale lilac petals make an attractive show. It can be used as a house plant, or it can be planted out in borders and window boxes.*

P. 'Deacon Moonlight'
ABOVE *Moonlight is difficult to describe, but these ruffled pale lilac pink flowers make agreeable heads of colour and do the name justice.*

MINIATURES

Because of their exquisite colour and form, miniatures make some of the best exhibition plants in the genus. Not surprisingly, their popularity is increasing formidably.

To BE A MINIATURE, as opposed to a dwarf, a pelargonium must be less than 12cm (5in). Micro-miniatures must be less than 5cm (2in) tall when mature. Miniatureness is a feature of variation. The more a group of plants is interbred the greater the chance that a miniature will be produced. As a result of interbreeding the first miniatures were noted at the end of the nineteenth century. The angel group of pelargoniums is thought to have originated through miniatures that were produced under artificial selection.

'Mini' pelargoniums, as they can be called, are also known from ivy-leaved, zonals and regals. There are six recognized categories: gold-leaved cultivars; ivy-leaved cultivars; paintbox or speckled cultivars; tricolor and variegated-foliage cultivars; stellars; and paintbox and speckled stellars. The flowers of miniatures may be single, semi-double or double. The shape of the flowers reflects their origins and if the flower does not hint at ancestry the leaves can sometimes help to determine the origin of the plant.

The National Collection of Miniatures and Dwarf Pelargoniums in England now boasts over 1400 cultivars – quite an increase in the 100 or so known 20 years ago. Many miniatures make superb show-type pelargoniums, including 'Morval', with its uniform balls of pink flowers, and 'Eileen' with its almost perfect balls of orange flowers. One of the most familiar of the miniature varieties is 'Red Black Vesuvius'. As a miniature it makes a bold statement in a window box or pot simply because of its unusual colour. It mixes well with other dark-leaved plants. Originally bred in 1890, it has remained a favourite ever since.

An unusual and unique miniature is 'Madame Salleron' AGM. It is a fancy-leaved pelargonium with attractive variegated leaves but no flowers. It

P. 'Black Vesuvius'
LEFT *Not a misnomer but a highly descriptive name for this popular miniature with dark foliage and strident red flowers. It performs well and makes a good feature in a border, window box, or patio pot.*

P. 'York Minster'

LEFT *As a dwarf this has variegated leaves in green and white, while the contrasting flowers are rosy red. The flowers are single and borne on small open trusses.*

MICRO-MINIATURES

These cultivars have a very tiny habit with reduced foliage and flowers. They look delightful in containers, either as a single feature or combined with other plants.

P. 'Playmate'

One of the hundreds of micro-miniatures that are now increasing in interest, this has tiny flowers with very thin petals.

P. 'Morval' AGM

LEFT *Awarded an AGM for its compact nature and double pink flowers with variegated leaves, this is ideal for exhibition or simply as a superb house plant.*

is a good grower and is therefore useful in foliage combinations. It does, however, produce a sport that has tiny pink flowers, called 'Little Trot'. 'Alde' shows off its orange flowers against a background of dark leaves and 'Friesdorf' has dark zonal markings. 'Greengold Kleine Liebling' (meaning 'Little Darling') has attractive green leaves combined with pink flowers which are borne on umbels. It is a more recent variant of 'Kleine Liebling' introduced in 1925. Fancy-leaved miniatures make good subjects in baskets and vases, including 'York Minster' and 'Caribou Gold' AGM.

There are many beautiful plants to choose from among the ivy-leaved miniatures. 'Alpine Glow' has a harlequin appearance in its bundles of pink flowers, 'Tenerife Magi' has unusual mauve semi-double and ruffled flowers, while 'Snow Queen' has purple traces on its pure white petals. Miniature cultivars of the continental-type cascades make exciting and unusual contributions to hanging baskets, creating lavender, pink or red mini-cascades.

Paintbox varieties have petals speckled with colours, often red or orange. The speckling can be over all the petals, or it may only affect one or two petals. 'Morse' and 'Shelley' are typical examples.

The interesting cut-petal effect of stellars has reached miniature status with some fascinating cultivars, such as 'Dawn Star', part of the Novelty range with pointed petals reminiscent of a cactus-flowered pelargonium, and 'David Mitcham'. In sharp contrast, 'Trudie' (listed as a dwarf) has elegant long, thin pink petals.

P. 'Madame Salleron' AGM
ABOVE *The attractive foliage dressed in green with irregular off-white markings makes this zonal pelargonium worthy of its AGM status. It can be grown as an herbaceous perennial, or as a house plant.*

P. 'Kleine Liebling'
LEFT *With the delicate pink blooms above the green and cream foliage, this miniature makes an attractive border plant or can be bedded in for the summer.*

P. 'Alpine Glow'
ABOVE *The flowers of this zonal double are white with red edges, and compacted to make an attractive flowering head of colour.*

P. 'Alde'
BELOW *A miniature with dark foliage and dark orange flowers, the petals are simple and constricted towards the base.*

P. 'David Mitcham'
ABOVE *The petals in this cultivar are finely divided so as to make the flowers quite unlike a pelargonium.*

P. 'Shelley'
ABOVE *With two-toned single flowers this dwarf has light upper petals and dark crimson lower petals veined with deep red.*

P. 'Flakey'
RIGHT *This is a very popular cultivar. The silvery green leaves are silver-edged and the small flowers are light mauve. The plant has a very dwarf habit.*

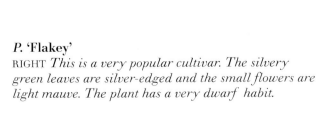

CULTIVATION

THERE IS NOTHING so satisfying for the gardener as propagating plants and watching them thrive. The following pages will show different ways of increasing your stock, and how to encourage them.

Many pests and diseases attack geraniums and pelargoniums, although pelargoniums have a natural line of defence. They have an effective range of deterrent scents, and their stems are covered in a felted armoury of fine hairs to ward off any would-be attacker. Geraniums are not so endowed with the means of resisting attack, but they are not so badly afflicted by pests and diseases.

G. sylvaticum 'Silva'
ABOVE *Cultivars of the wood geranium such as this one adjust well and will thrive in either formal or wilder borders.*

P. 'Beromünster'
LEFT *This is one of the many sports of* P. *'Royal Ascot', a small flowering regal or 'decorative' that makes an excellent features for large containers.*

GROWING AND PROPAGATING

Pelargoniums lend themselves to easy propagation. They have very obvious jointed stems and from one long stem a lot of new cuttings can be made. After only a few weeks a new plant can be raised from a short stem cutting.

THERE ARE MANY WAYS of increasing geraniums and pelargoniums. It is fast and easy to buy pelargoniums via mail order, either as seeds or as plugs. If you choose plugs the plants arrive in plugs of compost held together by a small net bag. The plants can be plugged into a large pot filled with compost. Some people prefer to snip off the netting, which can constrict some less vigorous plants, but if the plant is going to be discarded in the autumn there is no need.

Sowing seeds, f1 and f2 hybrids

Geraniums and pelargoniums set seed readily and these can be collected – although you must catch the ripe seeds before they are let loose. The pollen of one plant can fertilize another species. Seed for F1 hybrid single-flowered zonals is expensive but you are guaranteed reliability. F2 seed is less expensive but the color and uniformity are diminished. Seeds can be sown in seeding compost in open trays, or in vermiculite in closed see-through plastic boxes, which allow you to see the seeds while ensuring that they are given the right amount of moisture. Too much moisture can leave your seeds and seedlings prone to fungus attack.

Cuttings, layering, and dividing

Making cuttings replicates the plant you are taking cuttings from, and this is the way that most *P. × hortorum* (zonal) plants are propagated. One plant can produce scores of cuttings, which can be taken from the stem, tip of a growing stem, and from a leaf axil that includes the node from where the leaf or flower arises. Ensure that cuttings are made just below a node, so that roots can be stimulated to grow from this position. Always use a clean blade. The cutting should be made so that the segment of stem has a node from which leaf and flower buds will emerge.

LEFT *After a couple of weeks the new cutting or plant plug will be well established and will continue to grow rapidly under the right conditions.*

ABOVE *If you buy plant plugs by mail-order your plants will arrive packed securely in a box. For best results the plants need to be potted immediately and not allowed to dry out. Grown under ideal conditions before dispatch they need to be looked after carefully, especially under the right temperature regime. Do not order them too early unless you can cope with them indoors prior to planting out when there is no risk of frost.*

RIGHT *Taking a cutting is very easy. Use a sharp knife to cut a suitable growing tip that has at least one pair of leaves and one node just above the cut.*

You can buy compost for seeding and growing cuttings, or make a light growing medium at home using equal parts of sharp sand and home-made compost. Keep the compost moist, but it is better too dry than too wet. The ideal temperature is 23°C (73°F). Cuttings can be grown until there are at least two leaves, and then potted out.

Dividing geraniums is the quickest means of increase. Dig the plant up after flowering or during the dormant winter period and tease apart. One large clump can make many smaller plants. Try *G. endressii* AGM, *G. pratense*, *G. phaeum*, and *G. sylvaticum*. Pelargoniums are not suitable.

Some geraniums do not have large rootstock, such as *G.* 'Ann Folkard', *G.* 'Salome' and *G. wallichianum*, and cannot be divided. Take cuttings from their long stems and pot using a soil-based compost with grit. Other geraniums produce tuberous roots, and these can be broken off and potted. Layering can be employed in pelargoniums and geraniums, especially scented cultivars that are bedded out, or greenhouse plants. Long stems can be pinned down to allow the node to root.

Basic growing and maintenance

In Europe, Australia and North America plant out pelargoniums after the possibility of frost has gone. There are many cultivars that are continuously flowering from summer to early autumn. In America, plant out in the north when night temperatures are 16-18 °C (60-65 °F) and day temperatures are 21-29 °C (70-85 °F) – their optimum growing conditions. The high temperatures in Florida and Southern California restrain pelargoniums from flowering, so here it is best to make plantings in October and November.

Pelargoniums grow best in compost made from two parts loam and one part peat or leaf mould. Homemade compost is usually suitable, but digging pelargoniums into newly turned soil without compost is not advised. The roots prefer light and open soils with a little lime and some sand. Soil should be well dressed with some organic matter such as manure. Mulch the surface of the soil with grass clippings or tree bark chippings to improve water retention.

Water your geraniums and pelargoniums through the growing stage, allowing the soil to become almost dry. Water only to saturate the soil and allow to almost dry out again. If you use a high-pressure watering device be careful not to damage buds and flowers with water jets. Damage can also be sustained from heavy downpours, and hail.

Fertilizers can be applied weekly during the growing season, but cease during the winter. Do not supply too much nitrogen during the growing season since this can make the plant leggy.

In the growing season clear weeds from the base of stems, deadhead where necessary to encourage new growth and stop energy being wasted, and pinch out the growing tip to encourage branching out. When pelargoniums start to grow they can be shaped by pinching and cutting back.

ABOVE *Deadheading is essential to make the most of your plants. With a pair of pruning secateurs or a sharp knife cut the base of the old flowering stem and any discoloured leaves from the plant.*

LEFT *Pinch out the lead shoot to maintain a plant in shape. This is more important in a show plant than one in a hanging basket or pot. Pinching out stimulates the stem behind to produce more side shoots.*

PESTS

*Both geraniums and pelargoniums can fall prey to garden pests, such as caterpillars and aphids.
Geraniums are not as prone to problems as pelargoniums, but the scent and texture of pelargoniums can
act as a deterrent to would-be attackers.*

PESTS AND DISEASES are the scourge of almost all gardeners, and the geranium and pelargonium grower has to be prepared to deal with a range of problems. Fortunately pelargoniums have an effective range of deterrent scents, and their stems are covered in a formidable felted armoury of fine hairs to ward off any would-be attacker. Geraniums lack these natural defences, but fortunately they are not badly afflicted.

Caterpillars may eat both geraniums and pelargoniums. Despite the hairs and pungent scents of pelargoniums, caterpillars of various moths belonging to the *Noctuidae* family (noctuid moths) will eat pelargonium leaves, causing some localized trouble. This does not warrant any general control. Pelargoniums are not usually troubled by slugs and snails, but these pests may eat Geranium seedlings.

In Europe a relatively new pest of Pelargonium and Geranium is currently spreading its way northward from its origin in South Africa. This is the Geranium Bronze Butterfly (*Cacyreus marshalli*) which is a member of the *Lycaenidae* family (Blues and Coppers family). These are small insects and the wingspan of the Geranium Bronze is about 37mm (1 ½ in) wing tip to wing tip. The upper wings of both sexes are bronze, and the underside is silvery-black. It may be attractive but this little butterfly is something to look out for fluttering around flower trusses of pelargoniums in window boxes and containers.

The damage is done to the developing flower buds, since the adult butterfly lays her eggs into the cluster of buds. These hatch into small green caterpillars (larvae) with red markings that feed in

Whitefly damage
LEFT *The feeding whitefly leave marks on the leaves. These look quite innocuous but the damage leaves the plant open to infection.*

the buds out of sight. By the time the culprit has been found all the damage has been done to the developing flower shoot.

The widespread popularity of pelargoniums has provided the ideal opportunity for the Geranium Bronze Butterfly to spread, and to be transported from country to country as eggs and larvae in growing plants. It also feeds on members of the Geranium genus. The butterfly was first found in Mallorca in 1990, then in Brussels in 1991, in southern Spain in 1992 and in Italy in 1996. It has also been found in southern England. There is good reason to worry about the threat to nursery stock from this species.

The most serious insect pest of Geranium is vine weevil (*Otiorhynchus sulcatus*) although this is not a problem with Pelargonium. The adult is about 1cm (⅜ in) long and is dull black. It is nocturnal and feeds on leaves, eating telltale notches out of the side of the leaf. Its larvae, however, cause the most damage. The adult lays several hundred eggs and the larvae feed on the roots of the geranium. Out of sight, they are a particular nuisance in potted plants. In a large infestation a pot may contain scores of little white grubs. Clearing vine weevils from the garden may take several years since the insect is certainly fecund and very persistent. Washing the roots with water and applying a proprietary insecticide is highly recommended.

Both geraniums and pelargoniums are prone to attack by aphids and whitefly (*Aleyrodes* spp.). Attacks are more common when plants are kept in greenhouses and conservatories where conditions are so much more conducive to the build-up of populations. Given a lot of light and air and good drainage, vigorous plants can shrug off many potentially dangerous pests and diseases. Whitefly gather on the undersides of leaves and breed profusely. They are related to aphids and feed on sap taken from the undersides of leaves. Where they feed they leave a tiny mark on the leaf, which disfigures it and subsequently opens the plant to infection by viruses or fungal spores. The same is true for aphids, for the underside of infected leaves become pitted when there is a large infection. The remedy is to spray a proprietary product or to employ a biological control method, such as parasitic wasps or predatory mites, or using the fungus *Verticillium lecani* against whitefly.

Vine weevil

LEFT *The vine weevil is the arch-enemy of the geranium grower. The adult weevil (top) feeds on the leaves, while the larvae (bottom) cause havoc by feeding on the roots of the plant.*

Geranium Bronze Butterfly

ABOVE *This butterfly is now a common pest and a real threat to stock, especially that which is grown in a greenhouse or under glass.*

DISEASES

*Geraniums are not particularly prone to diseases, but both geraniums and pelargoniums can fall
prey to viruses and bacterial attacks, so it is important to know what to look out for.
Always deal with any sick plants quickly.*

VIRUSES ATTACK BOTH geraniums and pelargoniums, although it is often particular groups that are susceptible to diseases. In geraniums, *G. rubescens* and allies are attacked and leaves become distorted. Sick plants need to be burned and beware using seed from infected plants. Pelargoniums suffer from a number of viruses, as well as those described in the zonal section (see pp. 72–79) which are actively encouraged to produce exciting veining in the leaves. Crinkle or leaf curl virus causes wrinkling and deformity in young leaves, and the yellow net virus causes discolouration of the leaves. Virus-free stock is available in some countries.

The blotchiness of the leaves caused by these microscopic pathogens can be confused with the effect of over-watering in plants, especially the ivy-leaved pelargoniums. This condition is known as oedema where a build-up of water causes it to weep from the leaves. Very occasionally the stem

Rust
LEFT *Rust is
caused by a
fungal infection.
Patches of
brown spores
develop on the
underside of
the leaf.*

Galls
LEFT *Although galls do not seem to harm the plant,
they do make it unsightly. They only seem to afflict
some plants.*

Lack-of-water damage
ABOVE *Monitor your watering
regime to ensure that your plants are
taking in enough moisture.*

Virus damge to pelargoniums
ABOVE *Avoid using seed from infected plants as viruses can be spread that way.*

may be split as well. Little brown blisters eventually appear on the undersides of the leaves and make the plant quite unsightly. These occur after excess water has been forced out of the leaf, leaving a tiny brown scar. Collectively it looks like a disease, or an infection, and the best thing to do is remove the leaves. Avoid over-watering.

Lack of water can also cause leaf changes. As previously explained, water stress can cause a pleasing reddening of the leaves. A pittedness of the underside of ivy-leaved pelargoniums is also symptomatic of under-watering, and could be confused with slight aphid damage. Yellowing of leaves is a common indicator of a lack of watering, and can often be seen in nursery stock.

Fungi

Fungi attack both geraniums and pelargoniums, especially under glass where lack of ventilation, mist sprays and growing plants close together invites spores to run amok. The growing tips of plants succumb quickly to *Botyris cinerea*. Another fungus called Pythium blackleg, or black rot, causes new cuttings to go black and rot. Any plant infected with fungus or bacteria should be burned.

Bacteria

Pelargoniums are susceptible to galling, which fortunately does not spread. Galls appear at the base of the plant and multiply like green ant's eggs. The galls can be knocked off. Another bacterial problem is bacterial stem rot, which, as its name suggests, rots the base of the plant.

Fasciation can occur in many diverse groups of plants. This is a tendency of the growing part of the plant, generally the flower, to produce more cells than it needs, resulting in a bizarre shape to the flower. The cause is a mystery, but it could possibly be due to radioactive fall-out.

Mineral deficiency
RIGHT *This leaf discolouration indicates that the plant requires some mineral supplement.*

Drought
LEFT *Although lack of water can produce attractive effects, you should avoid buying water-starved stock.*

Oedema
ABOVE *Overwatering can produce leaf blisters that can be mistaken for a disease. Remove affected leaves and avoid overwatering.*

Fasciation
LEFT *What causes these flowers to become misshapen remains a mystery, but it could be linked to exposure to radiation.*

A-Z

THIS DIRECTORY OFFERS more than 175 species and cultivars of wild geraniums and pelargoniums from all around the world. They are listed alphabetically by Latin name, and the common names are listed where possible. The directory also includes information on flower and foliage colour, along with information on group, the flowering season and mature height.

Hopefully, the geraniums and pelargoniums featured in this book will have whet your appetite and will inspire you to try new species and cultivars in your own garden. In this directory there should be something for everyone.

P. 'Atomic Snowflake'
ABOVE *This scented variety has abudant foliage that will grow vigorously, so allow it plenty of space. It has delicate, mauve flowers.*

P. 'Tenerife Magic'
LEFT *These attractive mauve flowers of this miniature pelargonium will grace any window box or hanging basket.*

A-Z

*This comprehensive listing covers the most popular and attractive as well as some
of the more unusual varieties of geraniums and pelargoniums.
The flowering season runs from spring to late summer.*

GERANIUMS

G. **'Ann Folkard'** **AGM** cultivar, H60cm (24 in), magenta
flowers, green divided foliage mid season, sun and shade.
G. **'Dilys'** cultivar, H50cm (20in), red-purple flowers, cut-
leaved foliage, forms mounds, mid season.
G. asphodeloides species wild geranium (S. Europe),
H45cm (18 in), W30cm (12in) pale pink flowers,
early summer.
G. **'Birch's Double'** or 'Birch's Double Cranesbill',
cultivar, H30cm (12 in), double lavender flowers, mid
season, green to red foliage.
G. bicknellii **Bicknell's Geranium** (*G. longipes* and *G.
carolinianum* longipes), species (N.America), H45cm
(18 in), pale pink flowers, mid season, green foliage.
G. caespitosum species, purple flowers, H30-60cm
(12-24 in), mid season, foliage green and much divided.
G. canariense species (Canary Islands) red-purple flowers, H60cm (24 in), mid season, leaves dark green.
G. cantabrigiense species, compact pink flowers,
H15-20cm (6-8 in), green, early, fragrant foliage.
G. cantabrigiense Biokova Cranesbill', species, pale pink

flowers, H10-15cm (4-6 in), W 75-90cm (30-36in) early,
foliage green to red.
G. carolinianum Native to N. America, white or pale
pink funnel-shaped flowers, H15-38cm (6-15 in)
G. cinereum Ashy Cranesbill species (Pyrenees,
Europe), pink or white flowers, H15cm (6 in), early,
foliage grey.
G. cinereum **'Ballerina'** **AGM**, cultivar, light purple
petals, H20cm (8 in), green foliage.
G. cinereum **'Lawrence Flatman'** vigorous cultivar, pur-
ple flowers, H45cm (18 in), green foliage.
G. cinereum **'Splendens'** cultivar, bright magenta flow-
ers, H15cm (6 in), mounded, mid season, foliage green.
G. clarkei species (Kashmir, India), purple-violet or
white flowers, H50cm (20 in) tall, early-late season,
spreading silvery-green foliage.
G. clarkei **'Kashmir Purple'** cultivar, deep purple flowers,
H45cm (18 in), early-late season, foliage green spreading.
G. clarkei **'Kashmir White'** cultivar, large white and
pink flowers, H45cm (18 in), mid season, foliage green.
G. dalmaticum Dalmatian Cranesbill, species
(Dalmation mountains, Europe), pink flowers, H 15cm (6in)

G. Cinereum subsp. *subcaulescens'*

W50cm (20in), early-mid season, foliage green to red.

G. dissectum Cut-leaved cranesbill, species (Europe), pink flowers, H15cm (6 in), early-mid season, green foliage.

G. endressii AGM Western Cranesbill, species (W. Europe), soft pink flowers, H45cm (18 in), early summer-mid autumn, foliage light green.

G. endressii 'Wargrave Pink', cultivar, pink flowers, H45cm (18 in), mid season, foliage green.

G. erianthum, Woolly Geranium, species (N.America & Asia), blue-purple flowers, H20cm (8 in), mid season, foliage green.

G. esclliflorum 'Nigrans', cultivar, cream-white flowers, mid season, foliage black, H5cm (2 in).

G. gracile species (Turkey, Iran), pink and white flowers, 45cm (18 in), mid–late season, foliage green.

G. himalayense (*G. grandiflorum*), species (Himalayas, India), large lilac and purple flowers, H45cm (18 in), mid–late season, foliage green, autumn colour.

G. himalayense 'Gravetye' AGM, cultivar, lilac-purple flowers, H45cm (18 in), early-mid season, foliage green.

G. himalayense 'Plenum', (Birch Double) double violet blue flowers, H25cm (10 in), early season, foliage green.

G. ibericum species, (central Europe), violet blue flowers, H60cm (24 in), mid season, foliage green.

G. ibericum ssp *jubatum*, subspecies, blue flowers, H45cm (18 in), mid season, foliage green.

G. incanum species wild geranium (S.Africa), deep pink flowers, H45cm (18 in), early-mid season, foliage red and aromatic. Tender.

G. kishtvariense species wild geranium, deep pink-purple flowers, H24 in (60cm), mid season, foliage green.

G. 'Kurrodo' cultivar, purple flowers, H12 in (30cm), mid season, foliage pale green.

G. 'Johnson's Blue' AGM cultivar, large blue flowers H60cm (24 in), mid season, foliage green, sprawler.

G. 'Joy' cultivar, small pale pink flowers, H30cm (12 in), mid season, foliage green, groundcover.

G. libani (*G. libanoticum*) species wild geranium (E. Mediterranean), violet-blue or violet flowers, H30cm (12 in), early season, dormant during mid season, foliage green, evergreen.

G. lucidum species (south Europe, north Africa, central Asia), deep pink flowers, H60cm (24 in), early-mid season, foliage glossy green,

G. macrorrhizum Scented cranesbill, Big root Cranesbill (N. America), species, pink flowers, H37.5cm (15 in), mid season, dark green leaves, aromatic, groundcover.

G. macrorrhizum 'Album' AGM cultivar, white flowers, H60cm (24 in), early-mid season, foliage dark green.

G. macrorrhizum 'Chatto' cultivar, pink flowers, H60cm (24in), early season and mid season, foliage dark green.

G. macrorrhizum 'Ingwersen's Variety' AGM, cultivar, strong pink flowers, H60cm (24in), mid–late season, dark green leaves, scented, autumn colours.

G. macrorrhizum 'Spessart' cultivar, pale pink flowers, H37cm (15 in), early-mid season, foliage green, scented.

G. macrorrhizum 'Variegatum' cultivar, pink flowers,

H45cm (15 in), mid season, foliage cream and green.

G. maculatum Spotted Geranium, Storksbill, Alum Bloom, Alumroot, Wild Geranium, Chocolate Flower, Crowfoot, Dove's Foot, Old Man's Nightcap, Shameface, Madonna's Pins), species, pink flowers, mid season, H 35-70cm (12-30 in) foliage green, historical use as astringent and tonic.

G. maderense AGM species wild geranium (Madeira), purple red flowers, HW 100-250cm (36-60in), mid season, rosette, foliage dark green, biennial, tender

G. × magnificum AGM Showy hybrid, large blue-violet flowers, H60cm (24 in), mid season, foliage green.

G. malviflorum species wild geranium (Spain, Morocco, Algiers), violet blue flowers, H 60cm (24 in), early season, foliage green, good in rock gardens.

G. nodosum Knotted Cranesbill, species wild geraniums, bright purple-pink flowers, mid season, foliage glossy green, shady gardens. H 30-50 cm (12-20 in)

G. 'Nimbus' cultivar, magenta flowers, H 60cm (24 in), mid season, foliage green, ideal for shady areas and groundcover.

G. ocellatum species wild geranium (Africa to China), purplish-pink flowers, H60cm (24 in), mid season, foliage green, ideal for rock gardens.

G. orientalitibeticum species wild geranium (SW China), deep pink flowers with white eyes, H20cm (8 in), mid season, foliage green, rock garden or border. It can become invasive.

G. × oxonianum hybrid, pale pink flowers, H60cm (24 in), mid season, vigorous, clump forming, 'oxonianum' means that it pertains to the city of Oxford.

G. × oxonianum 'A.T. Johnson' AGM hybrid, silvery pink flowers, H60cm (24 in), mid season, foliage green, groundcover plant.

G. × oxonianum 'Claridge Druce' hybrid, pink flowers, H60cm (24 in), mid–late season, foliage green, vigorous, good groundcover.

G. × oxonianum 'Old Rose' hybrid, variable colour flowers from red-purple to dark purple, H30cm (12 in), mid season, foliage green.

G. × oxonianum 'Rose Clair' hybrid, satin rose coloured flowers, H45cm (18 in), mid–late season, foliage green, sprawling plant.

G. × oxonianum 'Thurstonianum' hybrid, small purple-red flowers, H 45cm (18 in), mid season, foliage green, enjoys both sun and shade.

G. × oxonianum 'Wargrave Pink' AGM hybrid, salmon-pink flowers, H24 in (60cm), mid season, foliage green.

G. 'Pagoda' hybrid (*G. sinensis* and *G. yunnanense*), dark purple flowers, H 45cm (18 in), mid–late season, foliage green.

G. 'Patricia' hybrid (*G. endressii* and *G. psilostemon*), bright magenta flowers, H 1m (36 in), early-late season, foliage green.

G. palmatum AGM species wild geranium (Madeira), purple flowers, mid season, foliage deep green, as rosette. H 120cm (48 in), tender.

G. palustre Marsh Cranesbill, species wild geranium (east and central Europe), bright magenta flowers, H60cm (24 in), mid season, foliage green.

G. phaeum Dusky Cranesbill, Mourning Widow, species, dark chocolate-coloured flowers, H60cm (24 in), mid season, good mixer, shade tolerant.

G. phaeum 'Album', cultivar, white flowers, H45cm (18 in), mid season, foliage green, shady position.

G. phaeum 'Lily Lovell' cultivar, lavender flowers, H30cm (12 in), mid season, foliage green.

G. phaeum 'Phillipe Vapelle' cultivar, purple-blue flowers, H30cm (12 in), mid season, foliage green.

G. phaeum 'Samobor' cultivar, flowers purple-blue, mid season, foliage green and chocolate.

G. platypetalum species wild geranium (E.Europe), purple flowers, H60cm (24 in), mid season, foliage green and hairy, mounds.

G. pratense Meadow Cranesbill, European species, violet-blue flowers, H60cm (24 in), early-mid season, foliage green.

G. pratense 'Mrs Kendall Clark' cultivar, bright blue flowers, H100cm (36 in), early season, foliage green.

G. psilostemon AGM species wild geranium (Armenia), bright magenta flowers, H100cm (36 in), early-mid season, foliage patchy light green

G. pusillum species wild geranium (Northern Europe & Asia), lilac flowers, H15cm (6 in), early-mid season, foliage green, annual, weedy.

G. pylzowianum species wild geranium (W. China), rose-pink flowers and green eyes, H 25cm (10 in), early season, green leaves.

G. pyrenaicum Hedgerow Cranesbill, species wild geranium (Europe), pink flowers, H30cm (12 in), mid season, foliage green, groundcover, invasive and weedy.

G. renardii AGM Renard's Cranesbill, species wild geranium (Caucasus mountains in Europe), flowers white with dark purple velvet veins, 40cm (15in), mid season, foliage green.

G. richardsonii species wild geranium (W. North America), pink flowers, H 30cm (12 in) mid-late season, foliage green turning red in autumn.

G. robertianum Herb Robert, Mary's Grace, species wild geranium (Asia, Europe, N.America), H 60cm (24 in), mid season, foliage green going red with season.

G. sanguineum Bloody Cranesbill, magenta-coloured flowers, 45cm (18 in), mid season, leaves dull green, mounded, once respected as a medicinal plant in Europe.

G. sanguineum 'Alan Bloom' crimson flowers, H 30cm (12 in), mid season, foliage dull green, sprawling habit, ideal for a rockery.

G. sanguineum 'Album' AGM albino flower form, H 30cm (12 in), mid season, foliage dull green.

G. sanguineum 'Cedric Morris' cultivar, rose-cerise flowers, H 30cm (12 in), early-late season, foliage green.

G.sanguineum 'John Elsley' cultivar, magenta flowers, H 20cm (8 in), foliage green, rockeries in full sun, sprawling habit, drought tolerant. All summer blooms.

G. sanguineum 'Glenluce' cultivar, reddish-purple flowers, H 60cm (24 in), foliage dark green.

G. sanguineum 'Max Frei' cultivar, pink flowers, H 37.5cm (15 in), mid-late season, foliage green, groundcover plant.

G. sanguineum 'New Hampshire Purple' cultivar, reddish-purple flowers, H 60cm (24 in), mid-late season, foliage green, mounded.

G. × riversleanainum 'Mavis Simpson' cultivar, purple-pink flowers with dark veins, H30cm (12 in), mid season, foliage green, rockeries and borders.

G. × riversleanainum 'Russell Prichard' AGM Cultivar, bright reddish purple flowers, H36 in (100cm), mid-late season, spreader, groundcover, rockeries.

G. sanguineum 'Nyewood' cultivar, flowers reddish-purple, H20cm (8 in), mid season, foliage green.

G. sanguineum var. striatum (*G. lancastriens*), cultivar, flowers pale pink flowers with striations, H 25cm (10 in), mid season, foliage green.

G. sanguineum 'Purple Flame' cultivar, purple flowers, H 60cm (24 in), mid-late season, foliage green.

G. sinense species wild geranium (SW China), black-maroon flowers, H30cm (12 in), mid-late season, foliage green and sticky; once used , late season, foliage green, nectar source to wasps and hover-flies, wild gardens.

G. 'Sirak' cultivar, flowers strong pink, H30cm (12 in), mid-late season, foliage green and sticky; once used , mid season, foliage green, full sun in border.

G. 'Spinners' cultivar, blue purple flowers, H30cm (12in), early-mid season, foliage green, groundcover.

G. 'Sue Crüg' cultivar, large pink flowers with dark veins running all over the petals, H30cm (12 in), mid season, foliage light green.

G. 'Syabru' cultivar, flowers violet-purple, mid season, H30cm (12 in), foliage green, vigorous.

G. sylvaticum Wood Cranesbill, flowers pink purple, H 45cm (18 in), early-mid season, foliage green.

G. sylvaticum 'Album' AGM albino flower form, H 45cm (18 in), early-mid season, foliage green.

G. sylvaticum 'Mayflower' AGM large blue flowers, H 45cm (18 in), mid season, foliage green.

G. sylvaticum f. albiflorum white flower form, H 45cm (18 in), mid season, foliage green.

G. sylvaticum 'Silva' cultivar, blue-purple flowers with white eyes, H 45cm (18 in), foliage green.

G. thunbergii species wild geranium (China, Taiwan, Japan) white to deep purple flowers and interesting blue anthers and red stigmas, H30cm (12 in), early to late season, foliage green, groundcover.

G. tuberosum species wild geranium (S.Europe) blue-purple flowers, H30cm (12 in), early-mid season, foliage green, rock garden, tender

G. versicolor species wild geranium (Mediterranean) red-purple flowers, HW 30cm (12 in), early-late season, foliage green, wild or woodland garden with shade; 'Snow White' has a more upright habit and is attractive in shady areas.

G. viscosissimum Sticky Cranesbill, species (N.America) pale lavender flowers, H30cm (12 in), mid-late season, foliage green and sticky; once used medicinally by native American to cure headaches.

G. wallichianum 'Buxton's Variety' AGM (also 'Buxton's Blue') cultivar, blue flowers with white centres, H30cm (12 in), mid–late season, foliage green.

G. wlassovianum species wild geranium (N & E Asia) magenta-purple flowers, H30cm (12 in), mid season, foliage grey and hairy, mounded, woodland gardens.

G. yoshimoi species (Japan) white flowers, H30cm (12 in), mid season, green foliage, white marbling.

PELARGONIUMS

P. alchemilloides species pelargonium (South Africa), with pink, white or cream flowers. Ideal as a pot plant.

P. appendiculatum a species pelargonium (South Africa), with yellow flowers. Ideal as a pot plant.

P. 'Atomic Snowflake' scented, a vigorous plant outside in a pot or in a greenhouse where it can take over. Its pale lavender flowers are pleasant additions to its abundant foliage.

P. 'Attar of Roses' scented with pale purple flowers. Can be grown outside, perhaps with other scented plants around a water feature, or sunken hollow where the scents linger.

P. barklyi species (South Africa) cream flowers.

P. 'Bird Dancer' AGM stellar group, a popular cultivar with pale pink star-shaped petals, an ideal mixer in a container or window box.

P. 'Bronze Corrine' zonal with salmon flowers and bronze foliage. Ideal for a window box.

P. capitatum The Rose Pelargonium, grows wild on Table Mountain in South Africa as a woody shrub. It is a favourite in the garden with its fragrant flowers and leaves. The plant is vigorous and the leaves are hairy and strongly lobed.

P. 'Captain Starlight' Angel with pink purple and white flowers, makes a good specimen in a hanging basket mixed with verbenas.

P. 'Carl Red Balcony' useful ivy-leaved pelargonium ideal for window boxes.

P. 'Cascade de Feu' trailing ivy-leaved pelargonium. with fiery colours, ideal for a window box.

P. 'Catford Belle' AGM classic Angel with contrasting pale purple flowers. Grow as a potted specimen or in a border.

P. 'Charity' AGM this has leaves of two colours, each with emerald green in the centre edged in lemon.

P. 'Chocolate Peppermint' AGM (also 'Chocolate Tomentosa'), scented, with chocolate-coloured marking and peppermint scent. Grow it, like other scenteds, outside close to a path so that the scents are disturbed on brushing past it.

P. coriandrifolium a form or species *P. myrrhifolium* with white to purple flowers.

P. crispum 'Variegatum' (syn. variegated Prince Rupert) scented, contorted leaves borne on an upright stems with green and cream leaves. Makes an attractive subject in a pot.

P. crithmifolium a species pelargonium from South Africa with white flowers.

P. cucullatum known as Wilde-Malfa in South Africa this is a shrubby plant which can grow up to 1m (3ft) tall. It has single leaves up its stem and it bears pink flowers.

P. 'Dainty Maid' decorative Angel with pale pink flowers. Grow it in a pot or in a border.

P. 'Dolly Varden' zonal fancy-leafed, cream-edged leaves and red flowers. Good in pots and window boxes.

P. 'Freak of Nature' zonal, scarlet flowers; parts of the plant have white stems and apple green marks on leaves. An eye-catcher wherever grown in pots and containers.

P. fulgidum a species pelargonium that has different shaped leaves and different coloured flowers or pink and red. For the specialist gardener.

P. glutinosum a species pelargonium. that has shiny and sticky leaves. Interesting as a curiosity.

P. 'Grand Slam' regal with rose-red to carmine flowers. Grow it as a potted plant within a patio feature, or bed out in a not-overcrowded bed.

P. grandiflorum a species pelargonium with leaves not entirely dissimilar to those of *Geranium sanguineum*. It flowers which are borne on long stems are white or pinkish with dark markings along the top two sepals. Like so many species, the leaves tend to become reddish with age.

P. 'Greengold Kleine Liebling' zonal, ideal with its decorative foliage in hanging baskets and window boxes. Means 'Little Darling', miniature.

P. 'Happy Thought' AGM often misspelled as 'A Happy Thought', hot red flowers.

P. 'Harlequin Mahogany' a single ivy-leaved with deep red flowers striped in white. Good in window boxes.

P. 'Harlequin Miss Liverbird' a single ivy-leaved with pink flowers and white stripes.

P. 'Highfields Appleblossom' large white-pink flowers with salmon centers.

P. 'Hills of Snow' zonal fancy-leafed, with green and white foliage and pale pink flowers.

P. inquinans a species pelargonium from South Africa, with red flowers, regularly grown as a houseplant or in conservatories.

P. 'Jacqueline' double red, part of the 'American First Lady' series.

P. kewensis a very attractive species pelargonium with large trusses of impressive bright red flowers.

P. 'L'Elégante' an elegant ivy-leaved pelargonium that has white flowers with a touch of pink.

P. 'Lara Maid' AGM decorative angel, ideal in pots, window boxes and hanging baskets.

P. 'Lavender Grand Slam' AGM regal. Grow as a potted specimen on a patio or by some steps for best effect.

P. longifolium a species pelargonium. from South Africa. Grows to about 20cm (8in) in height and has pink, white or yellow flowers borne above its finely-divided leaves.

P. **'Lord Bute'** AGM regal bute with carmine-edged violet flowers. Can be bedded out in hottest areas, otherwise it makes a good subject in a basket.

P. **'Madame Butterfly'** zonal fancy-leafed with silver variegated leaf and crimson flowers.

P. **'Mangel's Variegated'** hot red zonal with splashes of yellow on its green leaves, fades in full sun, therefore at its best in the shade where its colours remain bright and cheerful.

P. **'Marie Roper'** regal bute with lavender violet flowers stained in black. Grow it as a specimen plant in a pot.

P. **'Mrs Farren'** zonal fancy-leafed, green and cream leaves with red flowers. Ideal in a window box.

P. **'Mrs Henry Cox'** AGM zonal, fancy leaved, tricolor leaves and pale pink flowers. Ideal for use in a hanging basket.

P. **'Mrs Stapleton'** sold as a species, this has soft, downy grey green oval leaves with minimal serrations, and the flowers are borne on incredibly long stalks 14cm (5 ½ in) and again on large flower umbels 5cm (2in), twice as tall as the plant itself. The flowers are pink-red and last for a few days.

P. **'Mrs Strang'** zonal, fancy leaved with orange flowers, ideal for a window box.

P. myrrhifolium a species pelargonium which takes its Latin name from leaf shape. There is a variety which is also aptly named *coriandrifolium* – like the leaves of the umbelliferous herb, coriander. The plant is straggly in habit and bears relatively large pink flowers.

P. odoratissumum a species pelargonium with scented leaves, can be grown outside.

P. **'Paul Crampel'** this was propagated by the tens of thousands in the early 20th century and whose bright red blooms decorated many a window box.

P. **'Pearly Primrose'** regal pelargonium with attractive primrose colours. Grow it as a specimen plant.

P. peltatum a species from South Africa with white, purple or pink flowers. First introduced to Europe in 1700, the leaves were once used for deep blue dye.

P. **'Pink Gold Ears'** stellar group, the flowers are not as star-shaped as typical stellars, and the petals are broader on the pale pink flowers.

P. radula As its name suggests Radula radiates in all directions with its super-divided leaves that are a picture of filigree. Grow it as a potted plant outside in summer or inside during winter.

P. **'Rober's Lemon Rose'** scented, tall plant with mauve flowers and lemon scent, ideal around a water feature.

P. rodneyanum a species pelargonium with spear-shaped leaves rather like the shape of those of aspen. There are mild serrations around the leaves that are borne on long uncluttered stems. The flowers are equally stretched out on uncluttered stalks, typically 14cm (5 ½ in) and have a tight rosette of pink flowers.

P. **'Roi de Balcons Red'** a trailing pelargonium, ideal for a hanging basket.

P. **'Rouletta'** a classic pelargonium with great trusses of exciting flowers through the spring and summer, ideal in a window box, and can be supported to climb.

P. **'Royal Oak'** AGM scented, oak-shaped leaves, the plant grows well in pots during the summer.

P. **'Sancho Panza'** AGM decorative angel with pale-edge dark purple flowers.

P. schizopetalum, a species pelargonium from South Africa that has highly divided petals, as its name suggests.

P. **'South American Bronze'** AGM regal bute with white-edged bronze flowers.

P. **'Stadt Bern'** one of the hottest eye-catching reds of all the zonals, and can be used to form the basis of a special garden feature.

P. **'Startel'** stellar group, the trade name of a group of pelargoniums produced by Thompson & Morgan, 'Red Startel' being a typical example.

P. stenopetalum a species pelargonium with distinct leaves each with a definite dark zonal pattern. The flowers are borne on incredibly long stalks and are as big and bold as any ivy-leaf or stellar pelargonium in full flower. The flowers themselves have long spatulate petals of uniform design. A truly remarkable species that has great presence.

P. **'Susie Q'** zonal fancy-leafed, golden leaf with salmon pink flowers, perfect for a window box.

P. tabulare a smaller species pelargonium from South Africa with small pink flowers and leaves with dark zonal patterns on an ivy-shaped leaf.

P. **'Tricolor Hybrid'** a unique tri-coloured hybrid ideal for borders and boxes.

P. triste a species pelargonium growing as a loose rosette of finely-divided carrot-like leaves of dark green appearance. Could be employed in a black garden. Despite its sad name (*triste* means sad in french) it has an attractive inflorescence borne on a long hairy stem bearing yellow with brown-tinged flowers that produce one of the most intricate scents ranging from clove oil through incense to carnations, glue and joss sticks.

P. **'Turtle's White'** regal, large white flowers with frilly edges.

P. **'Vancouver Centennial'** one of the most widespread of zonals in the world, with amazing patterns on its leaves, it grows particularly well in the best Mediterranean climates.

P. **'Ville de Paris'** a trailing ivy-leaved pelargonium. Ideal in a hanging basket.

P. **'Wayward Angel'** AGM Angel with mauve and purple flowers, can be grown as specimen in basket or bedded out in warmer climates.

P. zonale the original species pelargonium from South Africa that has given its genetic material for the thousands of cultivars and hybrids of zonals now produced.

INDEX

General Index

USEFUL ADDRESSES

Most of the suppliers listed below offer online catalogs and ordering. While seeds can be sent anywhere, the importation of live plants or plant material requires special arrangements and not all suppliers will ship internationally.

Canadians importing plant material must pay a fee and complete an 'application for permit to import'. Contact:
Plant Heath and Production Division
2nd Floor West, Permit Office
59 Camelot Drive, Nepean, Ontario K1A 0Y9
Fax: (613) 228-6605
Website: www.efia-acia.agr.ca

Americans importing plants must also obtain a permit and pay a fee, Contact:
U.S. Department of Agriculture, APHIS
Plant Protection and Quarantine Permit Unit
4700 River Road, Unit 136
Riverdale, Maryland 20737-1236
Toll-free Tel: 1-877-770-5990
Website: www.aphis.usda.gov

Avant Gardens
710 High Mill Road
Dartmouth, MA 02747
Tel: (508) 998-8819, Fax: (508) 998-8819
Email: plants@avantgardensne.com
Good selection of cranesbills and pelargoniums

Chiltern Seeds
Bortree Stile, Ulverston
Cumbria LA12 7PB, England
Tel: +44 (122) 958-1137
Fax: +44 (122) 958-4549
Email: chilternseeds@compuserve.com
Website: www.edirectory.co.uk/chilternseeds/
Over 40 cranesbills and many pelargoniums

Davidson-Wilson Greenhouses, Inc.
Department 10, RR2, Box 168
Crawfordsville, IN 47933-9426
Toll-Free Tel: 1-877-723-6834
Toll-Free Fax: 1-800-276-3691
Tel: (765) 364-0556, Fax (765) 364-0563
Website: www.davidson-wilson.com
Every variety of pelargonium: fancy leaf, ivy, rosebud, novelty, dwarf and miniature, specialty scented, cascading and more. Ships worldwide.

Forestfarm
990 Tetherfine Road
Williams, OR 97544-9599
Tel: (541) 846-7269
Fax: (541) 846-6963
Email: orders@forestfarm.com
Website: www.forestfarm.com
Good selection of cranesbills. Ships to Canada.

Fraser's Thimble Farms
175 Arbutus Road
Salt Spring Island, BC V8K 1A3
Tel/Fax: (250) 537-5788
Email: thimble@saltspring.com
Website: thimblefarms.com
Rare plant specialist offers several dozen cranesbill varieties. Ships worldwide.

Geraniaceae
122 Hilcrest Avenue
Kentfield, CA 94904
Tel: (415) 461-4168
Fax: (415) 461-7209
Email: geraniac@pacbell.net
Website: www.geraniaceae.com
Specialty nursery offers hardy geraniums plus some angel- and pansy-faced pelargoniums. Will propagate plants on request.

Heronswood Nursery, Ltd.
7530 NE 288th Street
Kingston, WA 98346
Tel: (360) 297-4172
Fax: (360) 297-8321
Email: heronswood@silverlink.net
Website: www.heronswood.com
Well-reputed nursery offers several dozen varieties of cranesbill, many collected by the owners. No shipping to HI or FL.

Holt Geraniums
34465 Hallert Road
Abbotsford, BC V3G 1R3
E-mail: mholt@uniserve.com

Website: www.holtgeraniums.com
Over 1500 different pelargoniums, custom propagated. Ships worldwide.

International Geranium Society
IGS Membership, Dept. WWW
PO Box 92734
Passadena, CA 91109-2734
Society of pelargonium afficionados. Publishes *Geraniums Around the World* magazine. On-line resources, society gardens, email discussion group. Membership US$12.50.

Katie's Scenteds
6236 Bellflower Blvd
Lakewood, CA 90715
Tel: (562) 619-6266
Fax: (562) 437-4419
Email: rjjennings@earthlink.net
Website: www.katiesscenteds.com
Large selection of pelargoniums, hardy cranesbills and special cultivars. No chemical pesticides used. Southern states and international shipments require phytosanitary certificate.

Papa Geno's Herb Farm
11125 South 14th
Roca, NE 68430
Tel: (402) 423-5051, Fax: (402) 328-9766
Email: orders@papgenos.com
Website: www.papagenos.com
125 varieties of scented geraniums

Richter's Herb Specialists
357 Highway 47
Goodwood, ON L0C 1A0
Tel: (905) 640-6677, Fax: (905) 640-6641
Email: orderdesk@richters.com
Website: www.richters.com
Hundreds of pelargoniums and small selection of wild cranesbills; seeds, roots and plants. Ships worldwide.

Roslyn Nursery
211 Burrs Lane
Dix Hills, NY 11746
Tel: (631) 643-9347
Fax: (631) 427-0894
Email: roslyn@roslynnursery.com
Website: www.roslynnursery.com
Excellent selection of hardy geraniums.

Ships to Canada and overseas. AZ and CA residents require phytosanitary certificate.

Shady Hill Gardens
42W075 Route 38
Elburn, IL 60119
Tel: (630) 365-5665
Fax: (630) 365-5664
Email: suggestions@shadyhill.com
Website: www.shadyhill.com
Specialty pelargonium nursery featured on Martha Stewart Living has two Illinois locations.

Silver Hill Seeds
PO Box 53108
Kenilworth 7745
Cape Town, South Africa
Tel: +27 21 762-4245
Fax: +27 21 797-6609
Email: info@silverhillseeds.co.za
South African seed specialists offer a long list of pelargonium seeds and some geraniums.

Swanland Nurseries
Beech Hill Road
Swanland (near Hull)
East Yorkshire HU143QY
England
Tel: +44 (148) 263-3670
Fax: +44 (148) 263-4064
Email: swanland@aol.com
Website: www.swanland.co.uk/Nurseries/
Hundreds of varieties of pelargoniums by mail-order. Ships worldwide.

Theatrum Botanicum
PO Box 488
Laytonville, CA 95454
Email: thebot@mcn.org
Website: www.hepting.com/thebot
Good selection of unusual pelargoniums

Wrenwood of Berkeley Springs
Rt. 4, Box 8055
Berkeley Springs, WV 25411
Tel/Fax: (304) 258-3071
Email: wrenwood@intrepid.net
Website: www.wrenwood.com
Dozens of scented geraniums.

ACKNOWLEDGMENTS

I would especially like to thank to Mrs. D. Downey and Mr & Mrs Peter Stapley of Kent Street Nurseries of Sedlescombe, East Sussex for allowing me unrestricted access to their historic collection of pelargoniums and for guiding me through the vagaries of pelargoniums, Jennie Maillard of Usual & Unusual Plants, Hailsham in East Sussex were generous in permitting me access to her extensive range of geranium species, and both Vernon's Geranium Nursery in Cheam and Mr & Mrs Brian Sulman of Sulman's Nursery at Mildenhall in Suffolk, for allowing me to photograph in their collections. Thank you.

The quest for geraniums and pelargoniums has taken me to various places in the New and Old Worlds, and I would like to thank Lee Ann Feltwell in Pensylvania, USA, Barbara & Jack Marcinowski in Poznan, Poland and Jan Krampla for his help in Czech Republic. Photographs have also been taken in various private gardens in the USA, UK and France including those of M.& Mme Andre-Pierre Junot of Anduze in the Cevennes.

On production, I would like to thank the reassuring guidance throughout from Susan Berry, my editors Corinne Asghar, and Francoise Vulpe for Firefly in the USA, to Claudine Meissner, Anne Wilson for layout and design. My thanks too to Gina Douglas, Librarian at the Linnean Society of London for facilitating access to Carl Linneaus's herbarium specimens and other literature for which we acknowledge thanks for permission to reproduce such images. My thanks to Dr. C. Jarvis, the Botany Curator of the Linnean Collection at the Natural History Museum on the status of Linneas's specimens. Graham Pattison of the National Council for the Conservation of Plants and Gardens was very helpful in verifying pelargoniums of conservation concern, Thompson & Morgan for verifying old pelargonium names, and Elsner Pac Jungpflanzen in Dresden, GDR for claryfing some of the more recent trade names. I am very grateful to Mary Spink of Swanland Nurseries in East Yorkshire for generously checking the manuscript. Finally I would like to thank my wife for joining me in my enthusiasm for these genera and helping this project to reality.